SOUTHERN BOY COOKS

GOOD GRITS!

John C. Waters

Jim (middle) at work in the kitchen of the Fish House with his daughter Madison, 12

Great Southern School of Fish
Jonathan
Benriner
Turning
Slicer
(China)

SOUTHERN BOY COOKS

GOOD GRITS!

JIM SHIRLEY

Foreword by Randy Hammer,
Executive Editor, Pensacola News Journal

Edited by Jerry Gill and Cindy Hall

Director of Photography, Gary McCracken

Book Design by Michael Kenney

Cover Design by Cindy Hall and Michael Kenney

Copyright © 2005 • ISBN 1-59725-031-7

PEDIMENT PUBLISHING
A Division of The Pediment Group, Inc.

TABLE OF CONTENTS

*This book is dedicated to Cooper Yates,
the greatest publicist since "Swifty" Lazar.*

FOREWORD

I remember the first time I ate at the Fish House. My teen-age daughter took me there for Father's Day, and I was quite impressed she chose such a nice restaurant.

I was even more impressed when I looked at the menu. It wasn't the snapper and grouper and yellowfin tuna specials that captured my attention, but the list of Southern side dishes, which ranged from fried okra to collard greens to cheese grits.

The cheese grits weren't anything like my mother and father's grits.

These were Gouda grits, a dish flavored with the creamy, nutty taste of a smoked cheese from Holland.

This was my kind of place — seafood and Southern, but nontraditional Southern.

Fish House Chef Jim Shirley, I learned, is a Pensacola native. His restaurant's regional flavor centers on his belief that good cooking and good food start with the freshest local produce and seafood.

This translates into dishes such as pecan-crusted red snapper, where the fish comes from Pensacola waters, once known as the red snapper capital of the world, and the pecans from a local pecan company called Renfroe's.

The other thing I've learned about Jim over the years is that he likes to experiment. While the Fish House and its little-brother restaurant next door, the Atlas Oyster House, might specialize in Southern cooking, they also offer a melting pot of cuisines.

So in addition to fried oysters and hush puppies, you'll find on the menu such dishes as Asian pesto mahi mahi, Hong Kong crab cakes, and shrimp enchiladas.

On Tuesdays, Jim used to have what he called Thai night. I seldom missed it. And neither did Cooper Yates, who helped Jim design the restaurant.

Cooper was a Pensacola fixture who had owned several advertising agencies and

FOREWORD

dabbled in the publishing business. He and his business partners — Mike Kenney and Jerry Gill — went to work for the Pensacola News Journal and helped produce the Pelican, a biweekly newspaper that circulated in the Perdido Key area.

Cooper pitched the idea of a food column written by Jim that would be called Good Grits. Each column would feature a new recipe by Jim, and it would run in the Pelican and the News Journal.

I was lukewarm at first. Then Jim turned in a couple of columns. Lo and behold, the boy could write. More important, the boy could cook.

To be honest, I didn't think Jim could produce a recipe a week. That was three years ago, and Jim hasn't missed a deadline yet.

This cookbook is a collection of Jim's most popular recipes from his weekly column. The book, however, has one thing the column never touched, and that's the recipe for Grits à Ya Ya, the signature dish of the Fish House.

That dish alone makes this book worth the price of admission. I can promise you'll find other treasures inside, such as the Slow-Cook Chili on page 54, the Thom Kat Kai on page 73, or the Chicken Lulu on page 115.

Try a couple of those recipes Jim cooked up, and you'll have a good idea why folks here in Pensacola are fond of saying, "That boy can cook."

Randy Hammer
Executive Editor
Pensacola News Journal

From left, Fish House and Atlas Oyster House owners and partners, Will Merrill, Collier Merrill, Burney Merrill and Jim Shirley

INTRODUCTION

Welcome to my cookbook. Pour yourself a glass of wine, and I'll tell you how this cookbook came about.

I believe our histories are told by the food we cook and eat. This cookbook tells the story of my history, connecting my life experiences with the food I cook.

I spent my childhood traveling and eating with my family from Iceland to Australia as we followed Dad in his career as a Navy pilot. This book touches on that part of my life, but it focuses more on the great food and people I've met along the road as I revisit those traveled in my youth. In it, you'll get a feel for the crackle of fried okra in Grandma's skillet and see flashes in the woks of my Thai friends' grandmothers as we cook through their secret recipes.

So with my grandmothers' cast iron skillets, and a 99-pound sack of grits, I brought my taste for international cuisines home and began to mix local food – fresh produce from nearby farms and fresh fish from the Gulf of Mexico – and Southern cooking with flavors from around the world.

I hope you find the flavors of my life and cooking to your liking, and keep in mind the great wines that help complement our lives. If you feel the need to come looking for me, I've settled down in Pensacola, Fla., my hometown. With the help of my friends Burney, Will and Collier, I'm telling my stories daily in a couple of great restaurants on the waterfront in downtown Pensacola. We'll be looking for you.

Good Grits!

Jim Shirley
Executive Chef
Fish House and Atlas Oyster House

STARTS

The country road leading to Sweet Home Farm in Elberta, Ala.

SWEET HOME FARM FONDUE

Just across the state line, in Elberta, Ala., lies a countryside culinary jewel called Sweet Home Farm, where a family of cheese makers produces some of the best-tasting organic cheese in the country.

This Grade A dairy, with the help of a herd of Guernsey cows, produces and sells 16 varieties of all-natural raw-milk cheese.

These wonderful cheeses are worth the trip and are great for this spicy fondue. Try it with a bottle of Cellar No. 8 Merlot.

Sweet Home Farm Fondue

3 ounces Sweet Home Farm habanero cheese
8 ounces Sweet Home Farm garlic blue cheese
5 ounces Sweet Home Farm manchego cheese
1 tablespoon cornstarch
1 medium onion, diced
1 tablespoon olive oil
12 ounces Bass Ale
Bread cubes
Celery sticks
Carrot sticks
1 bottle Cellar No. 8 Merlot

Shred cheeses and toss with cornstarch. Sauté onion in olive oil until clear. Add beer to the saucepan, bring to a boil and slowly stir in the cheeses. Transfer to a warmed ceramic pot. Pop the bottle of Merlot and pour glasses all around, dip into the cheese pot and enjoy a little taste of home, sweet home.

OLIVES ANGELINA

Hey, when the entertainment season is in full swing, it's time to stock your fridge with goodies to throw out on the table when friends and family stop in. One thing that always works is the old-school relish tray, or antipasto. I recommend making a quadruple batch early in the season, which should last throughout.

This is a tasty recipe from Angelina Weller, first-generation Italian turned Southern. It's good with crusty bread and other foods, and great all by itself. But make a batch or two with peperoncino or mix in cheese from the assortment available from our friends at Sweet Home Farm. Chris Bilbro's Marietta Cellars Old Vine Red wines, with their rich fruit flavors, will suit everybody's taste.

Olives Angelina

1 pint kalamata olives
1 pint green olives (Shoreline Deli is a great source)
1 large yellow onion, sliced
4 tablespoons minced garlic
1 cup balsamic vinegar
1 cup extra-virgin olive oil
2 teaspoons dried thyme
3 teaspoons dried oregano
1 teaspoon red pepper flakes
12 turns black pepper mill
3 teaspoons kosher salt
Plenty of Marietta Cellars Old Vine Red

Except for the wine, slam all the ingredients together, stir gently, shove in the fridge and let sit for a few days. Then, when friends and family stop by, crack a bottle of Old Vine Red and salute Angelina and her wonderful olives. Keep a small bowl in the kitchen for yourself.

SHRIMP AND AVOCADO SALSA

Some like it hot. Some like it really hot. Hot is my grandmother's pepper sauce for greens. Really hot is Blistered Dragon, the habanero-based hot sauce my buddy Michael Boles concocts on occasion. He used to bottle it, licensing it as Burning Necessities. Nowadays he makes it for only the lucky few.

Boles, who is a college professor and renowned sculptor, has a 500-bottle collection of original hot sauces and a legendary recipe for shrimp and avocado salsa that he whips up for special occasions (gatherings of two or more). Better uncork a bottle of crackling cold Sauvignon Blanc to help cool the fires should you choose to take the habanero route.

The Shrimp

1 pound shrimp, peeled and deveined
2 tablespoons olive oil
2 tablespoons minced garlic
Salt to taste

Avocado Salsa

2 large avocados, peeled and diced
1 medium onion, diced
4 cloves garlic, minced
2 jalapeños, seeded and diced fine
   (for extra hot, use habaneros)
2 medium vine-ripe tomatoes, diced
1 red pepper, diced
1 poblano pepper, diced
1 cup chopped cilantro
1 lime for juice
1 teaspoon ground cumin
1 tablespoon prepared horseradish

Cumin Toast

French bread
Butter, room temperature
Kosher salt
Cumin, ground

Have a sip or two of wine and then mix together the shrimp, oil, garlic and salt. Sauté shrimp for about 4 minutes, or until their tails make a C shape; stuff into fridge. While the shrimp cool, dice the veggies, then scrape them into a big bowl along with the garlic, lime juice, cumin and horseradish.

Eat a shrimp to check seasonings. Then chuck the shrimp into the salsa and mix well. Slice and butter the bread, sprinkle with a smidgen of salt and cumin and bump into the oven. Gather your friends, pour the vino and tuck in.

DUCK LUMPIA

As one forays into the world of gourmet dishes, one often discovers delightful side roads to take with the "byproducts" of the journey. For example, I recently needed a rich duck stock to make a caramel sauce. Good duck stock takes a bit of duck fat and duck bones with a little meat on them (which means picking, not eating, the meat off the bones). Removing the tasty duck meat leaves the problem of what to do with it. This is where we detour to the following recipe.

I've always been a fan of the crisp little lumpia rolls from the Philippines, which are usually made from ground pork or beef, green peas, garlic — and carefully guarded secret family ingredients (that differ from family to family). An orange dipping sauce and a couple of bottles of Las Brisas (a refreshing Spanish white wine) will complete this great party appetizer. Makes about 16 crisp rolls.

Photo: Gary McCracken

Duck Lumpia

1 duck, whole

Kosher salt

1 cup white wine

2 cups water

½ cup diced onion

2 tablespoons minced garlic

1 tablespoon fresh ginger,
  peeled and minced

10 turns black pepper mill

1 teaspoon red pepper flakes

½ cup cooked green peas

2 teaspoons soy sauce

1 teaspoon sesame oil

16 or so thin 4-inch slices carrot

16 or so slivers poblano pepper

1 cup bean sprouts

1 package spring roll wrappers

Canola oil for frying

2 bottles Las Brisas

Orange Dipping Sauce

1 tablespoon duck fat

2 cloves garlic, minced

1 shallot, minced

1 cup chicken stock

1 cup orange marmalade

1 tablespoon soy sauce

Brine duck for 2 hours in 1 cup kosher salt to 1 gallon of water. Rinse well. Toss the duck into a roasting pan with 2 cups water and 1 cup white wine. Slide the lot into a cold oven, turn to 250 degrees and leave it for 2 hours. Pull the bird out, strain off liquid and refrigerate bird and liquid.

When the bird is cool, pick most of the meat off the bones and reserve bones for stock. Pull the fat cap off the liquid and reserve. Save remaining liquid for stock.

Chop the duck meat into ½-inch pieces. Drop 3 tablespoons of duck fat into a large sauté pan heated to medium high. Add onions and sauté until clear; then add garlic and ginger and sauté for 2 minutes. Crank in black pepper, pitch in red pepper flakes and green peas, add soy sauce and sesame oil; then the duck meat. Sauté, stirring till incorporated and heated throughout.

Better pop a bottle of Las Brisas to settle yourself for rolling. Place wrapper with a corner facing you, place tablespoon of mix in center, 1 strip each carrot and poblano and about 6 bean sprouts. Roll away from you, folding corners in as you reach them. Moisten the ends of the roll to seal it. Roll until all are done, then refrigerate (store one level only; do not stack).

To make the sauce, sauté the minced shallots and garlic in duck fat for 2 minutes; then add chicken stock, marmalade and soy sauce. Reduce by 1 cup. Reserve and allow to cool.

When you are ready to cook and serve the rolls, heat a ½-inch of canola oil in a sauté pan to about 350 degrees. Add a few at a time to hot oil and fry until golden brown all over. Drain on paper towels.

MOUNTAIN LAKE MUSHROOMS

I truly love the generosity of Southerners when it comes to sharing family recipes. Recently, I was at a tasting for French Chardonnays, where Shelby Daniels knocked me out with his grandmother's recipe for mushrooms. The Chardonnays paired perfectly with her recipe. I've got a hunch these mushrooms would pair nicely with anything, so I'm going to be making a batch to go with a big slab of prime beef and some Pinot Noir from Bethel Heights.

I had to add a piece of bacon to the recipe. It just didn't seem right to have a Southern grandmother's recipe without some pig in it.

Mountain Lake Mushrooms

4 pounds portobello mushrooms
1 piece of bacon
1 pound unsalted butter
1 quart port wine
2 cups chicken stock
2 cups beef stock
1 tablespoon ground black pepper
1 tablespoon dill
1½ tablespoons Worcestershire sauce
1 bottle Macon-Vergisson La Roche from Verget

Pop a bottle of Verget to get in a mushroom-cleaning mindset. Rinse mushrooms and remove stems. Tumble all the ingredients into a large pan, except the Verget, which is reserved for tumbling into your glass. Bring the batch to a boil, reduce to a simmer, put a lid on and let it go for 5 hours. Then pull the lid and let it go 3 to 4 more hours, or until the liquid is just below the level of the mushrooms. To serve the mushrooms, allow to reach room temperature.

VIETNAMESE-STYLE BLT

One of my favorite Vietnamese foods is rice-paper rolls. The ones at Tu-Do's on Davis Highway in Pensacola are filled with shrimp, vermicelli and lettuce and served with a spicy peanut sauce. In my quest to Southernize the world's cuisines, and after sampling a half dozen or so rolls, it occurred to me that the classic BLT, with a blue cheese vinaigrette for dipping, would be great wrapped in these delicious translucent wrappers. Along with a glass of Fess Parker Riesling, this is a fine start for a meal. Also makes a tasty snack.

Rice-Paper BLTs

8 rice-paper wrappers

8 pieces applewood-smoked bacon, fried and chopped

1 cup cooked vermicelli — al dente

4 romaine leaves cut into strips

8 leaves fresh basil cut into strips

1 large vine-ripe tomato, diced

1 bottle Fess Parker Riesling

Blue Cheese Vinaigrette

½ cup blue cheese crumbles from Sweet Home Farm

3 ounces balsamic vinegar

1 shallot, minced

6 ounces extra-virgin olive oil

½ lemon for juice

4 turns black pepper mill

1 teaspoon sea salt

Start out with a sip of Riesling to relax yourself for the job ahead. Break out grandma's skillet and fry up your bacon while the vermicelli cooks. When you've chopped the bacon and cooked the pasta al dente, throw them in the fridge to cool down.

Pour the balsamic vinegar into a small bowl, toss in the minced shallot, squeeze ½ lemon into it and dribble in the oil, whisking like crazy. Tumble in the blue cheese. Twist in four turns of your pepper mill, sprinkle in the salt and give it a good stir. Reserve.

Fill a pan larger than a single sheet of rice-paper with 2 inches of warm water. Get all your BLT ingredients together. Take a sip of wine to steady your nerves; then dip a rice-paper wrapper into the warm water for about 5 seconds. They tear easily, so be gentle. Lay the sheet on a damp cloth. Across the middle, align a row of bacon, then vermicelli, then rows of romaine, basil and tomato. Fold bottom ½ of wrapper over the filling, fold the sides in to make an envelope, and continue rolling gently to the top. Place seam down on a damp towel and repeat with remaining wrappers. Cover with a damp towel until ready to serve.

NEW YEAR'S BLACK-PEPPER PANCAKES

When the New Year rolls around, instead of watching fireworks and waiting for my sister to once again choke on the dime in the black-eyed peas, I'll be in the kitchen preparing a bite to eat and working on my midnight toast.

For luck, try these petite black-pepper pancakes, topped with lucky black-eyed pea purée and finished with salmon and horseradish cream, for the perfect New Year's cake. Then toast the New Year with an American sparkler, Gloria Ferrer Blanc de Noirs, made from red grapes. A great pick.

Photo: Gary McCracken

Black-Pepper Pancakes

2 cups Bisquick
2 eggs, beaten
2 cups milk
1 tablespoon black pepper
1 tablespoon butter
1 or more bottles Gloria Ferrer
   Blanc de Noirs

The Lucky Peas

1 cup black-eyed peas, fresh
   or frozen and thawed
1 tablespoon minced garlic
¼ cup diced onion
Dash olive oil
1 silver dollar for good luck
1 cup chicken stock

The Toppings

1 cup sour cream
¼ cup prepared horseradish
Dash fresh lemon juice
Salt and white pepper to taste
½ cup finely chopped green onion
6 ounces smoked salmon, slivered

To start, pop a bit of bubbly as the first volley toward the new year. Fling the onion and garlic, along with a splatter of olive oil, into grandma's hot cast iron skillet. Sauté on high heat for 2 minutes, stirring briskly, then tumble in the black-eyed peas and silver dollar. Follow with the chicken stock. Lower heat to a strong simmer and let this go for 12 minutes or until peas are good and tender. Allow to cool a bit, remove silver dollar (the beans now have the luck), cast peas into a food processor, purée and reserve.

Toss Bisquick, eggs and milk into a bowl and stir until most of the lumps are out. Pour out vintage-silver-dollar-size pancakes onto an oiled, hot griddle and cook till golden brown. Reserve these also.

Splash together sour cream, lemon juice, horseradish, salt and pepper. Just before the party, spread a spoonful of black-eyed pea purée on each cake and lay a sliver of smoked salmon on top. Finish with a dab of horseradish cream and a bit of green onion.

When the ball drops, break into a version of "Auld Lang Syne" (words below), pour the bubbly, pass out the New Year's cakes and toast to a great New Year.

Should auld acquaintance be forgot
and never brought to mind?
Should auld acquaintance be forgot
and days of auld lang syne?
For auld lang syne, my dear,
For auld lang syne,
We'll tak' a cup o' kindness yet,
For auld lang syne.

SHRIMP COCKTAIL
On a Bed of Green Tomato and Black-eyed Pea Chowchow

When chowchow came over to the States in the mid-1800s with the influx of railroad workers, it was a concoction of preserved orange peel in ginger syrup. By the time I tasted it at my grandmom's table in the 1970s, it had morphed into the pickle and mustard relish most of us know today. I thought I'd change it a bit more by adding some black-eyed peas and green tomatoes. The liquid from the chowchow makes a delicious poaching medium — perfect for giving shrimp a sweet, hot glaze.

Shrimp Cocktail

20 peeled and deveined shrimp, 16 to 20 count

1 head cabbage, chopped

2 cups black-eyed peas, cooked

4 cups rice wine vinegar

1 cup sugar

1 tablespoon honey

1 tablespoon sesame oil

2 tablespoons dry oriental mustard

2 teaspoons kosher salt

2 teaspoons turmeric

2 teaspoons red pepper flakes

2 teaspoons ground ginger

1 red pepper, julienned

2 sweet onions, julienned

1 stalk bok choy, chopped

4 green tomatoes, diced

1 bottle Kiwi Crossing Sauvignon Blanc

Refrigerate wine.

In a large pot, over medium heat, simmer vinegar, sugar, honey, sesame oil and spices for 10 minutes. Toss in cabbage, black-eyed peas, red pepper, onions, bok choy and tomatoes. Bring to a boil. Reduce heat and cook for 8 minutes. Allow chowchow to cool, then refrigerate for at least 2 hours.

To serve, strain off 1 cup of chowchow liquid, pour into a sauté pan and bring to a boil. Lightly salt shrimp and toss them in the pan for about 3 minutes, or until they turn pink and curl into a C shape. Fill martini glasses halfway with chowchow, hang several shrimp off the rim of each glass, pour crackling cold wine all around, and chowchow down.

LEMON-THYME CHICKEN WINGS

Here I offer an alternative to the spicy wings that are the usual ballgame fare. These wings are especially tasty if you're sipping a light wine. The big tricks are to brine the chicken, stuff the seasoning under the skin, cook with the skin on, whether you eat it or not, and weighting the meat in the sauté pan, as you do when making Chicken Diavolo. The tartness of the light Las Brisas Spanish White makes it a dynamite choice with this chicken.

Lemon-Thyme Chicken Wings

5 pounds large chicken wings

1 cup kosher salt

3 quarts water

3 tablespoons fresh thyme (leaves only)

1 tablespoon dill

6 tablespoons olive oil

10 turns fresh-cracked pepper

4 cloves garlic, minced

4 lemons, halved

1 brick (wrapped in foil)

2 bottles Las Brisas Spanish White wine

Brine chicken wings for 3 hours in a solution of 1 cup kosher salt to 3 quarts water. Drain, rinse well and pat dry.

Tumble thyme leaves, dill, garlic and pepper with 2 tablespoons olive oil. Use a paring knife to open a pocket under the skin of each of the wings and slip this mixture in. Drizzle 2 tablespoons of the remaining olive oil into a large frying pan and heat to medium high. Dump in ½ of the wings and form a single layer. Place a lid, slightly smaller than the pan, on top, and weigh the wings down with a brick. Cook for about 15 minutes, then turn the wings and replace lid and brick. Cook for another 10 minutes. Repeat with the remaining wings. Pour everybody more wine, squeeze lemon over wings and serve hot.

COLLARD AND ARTICHOKE DIP

The other day I was cooking up a batch of collard greens my usual way, with plenty of ham and onions and a little garlic, and I remembered that someone had requested spinach and artichoke dip for a party that evening. Rather than making the usual, I substituted pot liquor for chicken stock, collard greens for spinach and Gouda for white cheddar.

Alois Lageder Pinot Grigio goes great with this tasty dip.

Collard and Artichoke Dip

2 cups cooked collards
12 ounces artichoke hearts
¼ pound butter
¾ cup diced onions
3 tablespoons minced garlic
¼ cup flour
1½ cups pot liquor

2 cups heavy cream
¾ cup sour cream
¾ cup shredded Romano cheese
1½ cups shredded smoked Gouda cheese
1 lemon for juice
1 teaspoon of your favorite hot sauce
1 bottle Alois Lageder Pinot Grigio

Sauté onions in butter over medium heat until translucent. Toss in the garlic and sauté for 1 minute. Sprinkle flour on top and cook for 3 minutes, stirring the whole time. Pour in the pot liquor and cream and bring to a boil. Add sour cream, and heat to steaming. Spread Romano and Gouda cheeses across top and stir until cheese is incorporated. Toss in the artichoke hearts and collards, squeeze the lemon in and add the hot sauce. Cook until everything is heated up and serve with toasted bread or chips.

For those of you in the anti-bread group, use sliced cheese for dipping.

BARB BUGGY'S FLAT BREAD

There's a space in Australia called the Barossa Valley, the heartland of the country, where farmers and winemakers work the soil of their ancestors' farms. These are not the croc-chasing outback types, but rather the steady farmers that remind me of my grandparents and their dedication to the land.

One such family is the Angases. They invited me to their ranch in Hutton Vale just outside Barossa. On their ranch, which their ancestors settled 160 years ago, the Angas family raises sheep, grows wine grapes, vegetables and even the nuts they eat. Deep believers in the slow-food movement, everything they served was from their land: Hutton Vale dry Riesling wine, roasted fresh almonds and pistachios, fresh hand-ground lamb sausage rolls, fresh-baked flat bread, an assortment of chutneys made with everything from spicy pumpkin to apricots and individual potato-lamb pots with garden vegetables (beans, bok choy, peppers). This feast, paired with wines from some of the best grapes in Australia and the incredible Aussie hospitality, made for a meal to remember.

Barb's Flat Bread

10 grams (.35 ounces) yeast

Pinch sugar

1 liter (1.06 quarts) lukewarm water

1 kilogram (2.2 pounds) baker's flour

Pinch salt

Splash olive oil

Pinch each fresh rosemary, thyme, sea salt and black pepper

1 bottle Hutton Vale Riesling

Preheat oven to 450 degrees. Combine yeast and sugar in a cup of the warm water. Let sit a bit before combining with remaining water. Mix a pinch of salt with flour, splash in the oil and stir in the water. Knead for a few minutes. Let rest 1 hour or until doubled in size. Knock down, divide into balls, roll out and make indentations around the edges with your fingertips. Top lightly with fresh rosemary, thyme, sea salt and black pepper. Bake for about 20 minutes. Crack a bottle of Hutton Vale Riesling and settle back with your local late-summer vegetables, the hot flat bread and your favorite chutney. If you don't have chutney, a marinara or an onion relish works great.

SHRIMP-STUFFED CHICKEN WINGS

When I visit Tu-Do, a local Vietnamese restaurant, I always order a few stuffed chicken wings. I'm not sure what they stuff the wings with, but I stuff mine with some fresh shrimp, ginger and garlic mixed with Jimmy Dean sausage in what I call Far East meets Deep South. Whitehall Lane Sauvignon Blanc complements this international concoction.

Photo: Gary McCracken

Chicken Wings

4 pounds large chicken wings
2 quarts water
2 cups salt
Seasoned flour
Panko (Japanese) bread crumbs
Canola oil for frying
Soy sauce
Marmalade
Hot chili oil
1 bottle Whitehall Lane
    Sauvignon Blanc

Seasoned Flour

1 cup all-purpose flour
2 tablespoons garlic powder
2 tablespoons onion powder
2 teaspoons white pepper
1 tablespoon ground rosemary
1 tablespoon salt

Egg Wash

1 egg
1 cup buttermilk

Stuffing

1 pound Jimmy Dean sausage (hot)
½ cup diced scallions
¼ cup minced garlic
¼ cup minced shallots
¼ pound diced shrimp
2 tablespoons sesame oil

Pitch the wings (joints and all) into 2 quarts water with 2 cups salt stirred in. Toss Mr. Dean's finest into a skillet over medium heat and brown. Then toss scallions, garlic, shallots, shrimp and sesame oil in with the sausage and cook till the shrimp go pink; about 3 minutes. Scrape everything in the pan into a food mill and mince very fine. Let this rest for about an hour — long enough to beat the egg and buttermilk to make the wash, season the flour, let the chicken soak for awhile and still have enough time to enjoy a glass of wine.

Rinse wings well; pat dry. Then, using a sharp, thin knife, run the blade down the fat side of the two large joints of each wing, opening a pocket between the flesh and the skin, and squeeze stuffing in till the skin is about to pop. Roll in seasoned flour, coat with egg wash and roll in bread crumbs. Fry in canola oil until brown. Pour wine for your guests, and serve the stuffed chicken wings with small bowls of soy sauce, marmalade and hot chili oil on the side so that guests can mix their own sauce.

FRIED BRIE

When I lived in Davis, Calif., my favorite place to spend a Saturday afternoon was the courtyard of the California Cafe. My fare of choice was fried brie and Caymus Zinfandel. Although Caymus no longer makes the wine, in nearby Morisoli Vineyard, Elyse is producing a fine Zinfandel.

Fried Brie

1 loaf French bread
1 wedge brie (hard frozen)
1 cup oil for frying
1 egg
½ cup buttermilk
½ cup all-purpose flour
1 tablespoon garlic powder
1 tablespoon onion powder
2 teaspoons salt
1 teaspoon white pepper
½ cup seasoned bread crumbs
2 teaspoons dried rosemary
1 bottle Elyse Zinfandel, Morisoli Vineyard

Heat your oil to medium high in a sauté pan or skillet. Make a wash by whisking egg in buttermilk. Thoroughly mix flour, garlic and onion powders, salt and pepper. Stir rosemary into bread crumbs. Remove brie from freezer and roll through seasoned flour, dip into egg wash, then coat with bread crumbs. Fry quickly — about 2 minutes on each side. Serve with fresh French bread and a bottle of Elyse Zinfandel.

PICI WITH MUSHROOM RAGU

In Pienza, Italy, I ate pici for the first time at Latte de Luna, a little trattoria well-known for the way they make it. Pici is a great-tasting, handmade pasta and a favorite in the area.

My thanks to Ken Ford, one of my dining companions, for introducing me to Latte de Luna's legendary fare. Ken's descriptions of the trattoria's suckling pig, duck with olives, and, of course, the local pici, were so enticing that we changed our reservations three times, and were scolded: "First there were only two of you, then four, now six! What will you people ask for next? There's no more room!" But once our group was ensconced within the tiny place, all was well.

That night they served the pici with a dark tomato-and-mushroom sauce. The Tuscan dish, rich and earthy, made us feel at home. I'm giving my best "Southern Boy Cooks Italian" shot at this recipe. You have to sacrifice a bottle of good red wine to make the ragu taste its best, but a bottle of Gundlach Bundschu Block 13 Pinot Noir for yourself will help erase the guilt.

Photo: Gary McCracken

Pici

1½ cups semolina flour
1 teaspoon porcini mushroom powder
2 teaspoons salt
2 eggs
2 tablespoons extra-virgin olive oil
2 tablespoons water
1 quart chicken stock
1 teaspoon vegetable oil

Ragu

2 tablespoons extra-virgin
  olive oil
2 medium red onions, diced
1 tablespoon minced garlic
1 teaspoon dried oregano
1 teaspoon dried thyme
1 tablespoon parsley flakes
1 pinch red pepper flakes

1 slice bacon
1 bottle red wine
2 28-ounce cans diced tomatoes
8 portobello mushroom caps, diced
Chopped green onions and shaved
Romano cheese for garnish
1 bottle Block 13 Pinot Noir from
  Gundlach Bundschu

Start the pici my mixing flour, mushroom powder and ½ the salt (1 teaspoon) together, then beat the eggs and toss into flour mixture along with the extra-virgin olive oil and water. Mix with a fork for a minute or so, knead the dough a few minutes, cover with a wet towel, and put the dough somewhere warm while you make the sauce.

Measure 2 tablespoons olive oil into a medium-size saucepan and heat to medium high. Dump in onions; when they're translucent, pitch in garlic, oregano, thyme, parsley, red pepper flakes and bacon. Sizzle for 2 minutes, then pour in the wine and tomatoes (including liquid) and turn on high. If you have any room left in your pot, toss in the mushrooms; otherwise, wait till the lot cooks down a bit. Stir now and then.

Finish the pici by firing up a quart of chicken stock in a medium-size pot. Add 1 teaspoon vegetable oil and 1 teaspoon salt. While waiting for it to boil, find a flat surface and roll out the dough until it's ¼-inch thick. Cut into ½-inch strips. Drop into the stock and let it roll about 10 minutes, but to be sure the pici's done, pull out a piece and taste it. You're good when it's not mealy in the center.

Remove, drain, and toss with a dollop of olive oil. Reserve. Keep the chicken stock rolling until reduced to ½ cup, then pour it in with the sauce, which should be thick and dark. Stir and remove from heat. Grab a large sauté pan and toss in pici, turn to medium heat and cover with enough sauce to thoroughly coat it. Tong onto plates, add a big spoonful of the sauce in the center of each, garnish with shaved Romano and green onions, pour wine for all, and gorge yourselves on a mighty fine feast.

SOUTHERN SIDES

Rodney Lewis shells peas at Bailey's Farmers Market in Pensacola

A MESS O' GREENS

A quick glance at the car tags down by the water will tell many a local that our friends from the North have flown the coop and are in L.A. (Lower Alabama) mode. To help you mix with the locals and warm your cold bones, Dr. Jim prescribes a heapin' mess o' greens.

A Mess O' Greens

5 pounds frozen collard greens
   (or 2 bunches fresh)
½ pound ham pieces or bacon
1 large onion, diced
1 small red bell pepper, cored and sliced
¼ cup hot sauce

1 tablespoon vinegar
2 tablespoons brown sugar
2 teaspoons black pepper
1 tablespoon (or so) salt
1 quart (or so) cold water

Here's the short of it. Grab the greens from the grocery or farmers' market — 2 large fresh bunches (and they are large), or 5 pounds frozen. You'll need a big pot if you're cooking fresh collards. I like to wash them in a large sink, soaking and shaking them in cold water till the grit rinses out of the crevices.

Chop into 1-inch strips so they'll "hang off your fork" when done.

From here on out, think collard soup. Start with some of that miraculous animal, the pig. Brown the pork in your pot. If by mischance your pork is lean, make sure you have enough vitamin G to sauté the onion till translucent.

Now toss everything else into the pot, including all the collards that will fit. Start with a quart or so of cold water; bring it to a boil. If you're cooking fresh collards, you're going to have to wait until about ½ are wilted in the pot before the rest will fit. Cook the greens down some, then add enough water to cover. Lower the heat and simmer for 36½ minutes, or until tender. Add as much salt as your ticker can stand and get ready to dine.

Now, I hope you have pepper sauce on hand and some cornbread to sop up the pot liquor, or everybody will know for sure that you're not from around these parts.

GRANDMA'S CORNBREAD

In the South, you'll find dozens of cornbread recipes, but every true Southerner knows the only correct way to cook 'em all: in a well-seasoned cast iron skillet. I use my grandmother's recipe — and the cast iron skillet she left me — to make this Southern staple. Everything I cook in that old skillet tastes better. I figure it's because she put 90 years of love into seasoning it.

Grandma's Cornbread

2 cups cornmeal (Martha White yellow self-rising)

1 cup all-purpose flour

½ cup sugar

1 teaspoon salt

½ teaspoon black pepper

2 eggs, beaten

¼ pound melted butter

1 cup buttermilk

1 cup sour cream

4 scallions (chopped, green tips only)

¼ cup chopped jalapeños

6 slices applewood-smoked bacon

1 bottle Hazy Blur Shiraz

Start out by opening a bottle of Hazy Blur Shiraz to prepare the way for some comfort food and possibly cancel the effects of at least 1 of the slices of bacon.

Mix all dry ingredients in a bowl. Stir in eggs, butter, buttermilk, sour cream, scallions and jalapeños.

Lay out bacon in rows in your grandma's cast iron skillet and cook till done. Pour mix into the hot pan over bacon; don't lose juices. Slide skillet into a 425-degree oven. Relax with a glass of Shiraz for about 20 minutes, or until a toothpick inserted into the middle of the baking cornbread comes out clean.

To serve, flip the bread over onto a serving platter so the bacon comes out on top. At my house, this is considered a whole meal: fruit in your glass, veggies from your jalapeños, grain in the bread, dairy in the milk and eggs, and a little fat and protein in the bacon.

DISASTER-PROOF CRAWFISH AND TASSO DRESSING

Every family has a collection of Thanksgiving mishaps that, over time, become tall tales and fables. When that day of American feasting arrives, here are a few lessons I've learned from the Shirley family history of Thanksgiving cooking glitches:

Always remember to turn on the oven that your turkey is in; it takes forever to cook a turkey at room temperature. Also remember to not use the broiler feature on the sweet potato casserole with the marshmallows on top. The marshmallows are flammable, and trying to beat the fire out with a towel just spreads the sweet napalm. Cats can be sneaky; keep them out of the house while you're cooking. And a word of caution to the gourmet cook experimenting with hot peppers; I have found that children and grandparents are not overly fond of chipotle, habanero or Thai chilies in anything.

That aside, this is a one-pan dressing that's disaster-proof if you don't forget to turn the oven on.

Crawfish and Tasso Dressing

1 pound crawfish tails
¼ pound butter
1 cup chopped tasso
1 cup celery, diced
1 cup onion, diced
1 medium carrot, diced

2 cloves garlic, minced
2 shallots, minced
¼ cup chopped parsley
1 pinch red pepper flakes
1 teaspoon tarragon
1 teaspoon savory

1 teaspoon thyme
1 teaspoon oregano
½ teaspoon salt
2 cups chicken stock
4 cups fresh bread crumbs
1 bottle Pinot Noir

Photo: Gary McCracken

The Pinot Noir isn't an ingredient in this recipe; it's simply the best wine to drink when it's time to eat this delicious dressing and the turkey, ham and all the usual trimmings. And it is perfect to sip on while cooking, so pour yourself a glass.

Preheat oven to 350 degrees. Toss the butter, tasso, celery, onion and carrots into grandma's cast iron skillet and sauté for 5 minutes. Add garlic, shallots, parsley and spices. Sauté for 3 minutes. Toss in crawfish tails, sauté for 1 minute, then pour in the chicken stock and reduce for 5 minutes. Now fold in the bread crumbs, slide the whole thing into the oven and bake for 15 minutes. Serve with the Pinot Noir and the rest of your Thanksgiving fare.

MACARONI AND CHEESE WITH BACON AND SHRIMP

Sometimes, when your world gets crazy, there's nothing like some old-fashioned comfort food to put everything back into perspective.

My No. 1 comfort food has always been Mom's made-from-scratch macaroni and cheese. I'll start with her recipe, then add a little touch of bacon and some Cajun barbecue shrimp to make it kick. This goes great with a Pinot Gris from Dr. Loosen.

Photo: Gary McCracken

Macaroni and Cheese

8 cups cooked macaroni

2 cups sauce

2 cups shredded cheddar cheese

1 bottle Pinot Gris from Dr. Loosen

Sauce

¼ pound butter

³/₄ cup all-purpose flour

2 cups milk almost at a boil

White pepper and kosher salt to taste

2 cups shredded cheddar cheese

Topping

³/₄ cup cornbread crumbs

³/₄ cup shredded
   cheddar cheese

2 ounces melted butter

16 slices fried bacon,
   chopped

Garnish

32 Gulf shrimp, peeled and deveined

¼ pound butter

¼ cup Worcestershire sauce

1 tablespoon Louisiana hot sauce

½ lemon for juice

1 tablespoon minced garlic

1 teaspoon kosher salt

2 teaspoons cracked black pepper

Juggling the macaroni, bacon and milk while you're making the sauce is the hard part of this recipe. Start by slowly warming the milk in a saucepan, boiling the macaroni and frying the bacon.

To make the sauce, melt butter in a saucepan at medium high, add flour and stir briskly for 7 minutes. The mix should be blowing hot bubbles from about 4 minutes on; at 7 minutes start whisking in the hot milk. Whisk for 3 minutes, add a little salt and white pepper to taste, then reduce heat and cook until the flour taste has disappeared. Fold in 2 cups shredded cheddar cheese. Stir until melted. Toss drained macaroni into a large bowl with 2 cups cheese sauce and 2 cups shredded cheddar. The tough part is over; have a sip of wine.

Butter a 9- by 11-inch baking pan. Fill bottom of pan ½-inch deep with macaroni mix; then top with ³/₄ of the chopped bacon. Add remainder of macaroni. Toss cornbread crumbs with the remaining bacon and 2 ounces of melted butter. Sprinkle over macaroni. Bake 15 minutes at 350 degrees. While that's cooking, prepare garnish: Warm grandma's skillet over medium-high heat; toss butter, Worcestershire, hot sauce, lemon juice, garlic, salt and pepper into the skillet. Stir and cook for 2 minutes after the butter melts. Pitch in the shrimp; cook until their tails start to curl. Flip shrimp and cook for about 2 more minutes.

Plate with a mound of macaroni and cheese in the middle, sprinkle with shredded cheddar and garnish with shrimp. Drizzle some of the remaining sauce over the shrimp. Call your company to the table, pour the wine and toast those golden days of yesteryear.

RED BEANS AND RICE

Mardi Gras parading is tough work: grueling hours sipping adult beverages on floats, followed by more of the same at Mardi Gras balls. You need lots of energy to fuel your bead-tossing. Red beans and rice are the historic staple of choice to help get you through the day — and night. Any day or night.

This is a small-batch, slow-cook interpretation of my friend Charlie Switzer's recipe. Each year, Charlie makes great-tasting red beans in 50-gallon kettles and serves 'em up free to thousands of Pensacola Beach revelers.

The following recipe probably doesn't vary that much from Charlie's except in the math. If you expect a crowd, just multiply by 400.

Red Beans and Rice

1 pound dried red beans
4 cloves garlic, minced
2 shallots, minced
1 small onion, diced
1 pound Thompson's beef sausage, ¼-inch slices (or ham hocks, ham bones, or anything else from that wonderful animal)

1 tablespoon hot sauce
2 teaspoons salt
1 teaspoon black pepper
1½ quarts water
Cooked rice

The night before the big day, rinse and soak beans, dice veggies and slice sausage. Next morning, put the veggies, sausage (or other meat) and hot sauce into a slow cooker; drain the beans and shake them into the pot. Add about 1½ quarts water, put the lid on and set cooker on low heat.

When you get home from work, crank cooker to high heat and start a batch of white rice. Give the beans a good stir to wake them up, crushing some against the pot to help thicken the sauce. Let it run on high for about half an hour, stirring and crushing until the sauce thickens. Salt and pepper as much as your ticker allows, spoon rice into big bowls, then ladle beans on top. Make sure you have lots of good hot sauce around, and something to drink to cool you down.

RISOTTO BARRACKS STREET

In keeping with my predilection to Southernize ethnic dishes, I present my version of the classic Italian dish, risotto, with my souped-up broth, which, when added at just the right time, will produce a marvelous creamy stew. Risotto has a reputation for being difficult to make, but with the following tips, you'll find it easy to add to your repertoire. Just think of it as rice that makes its own gravy.

Risotto is made with Arborio rice, a short, fat, starchy grain that really absorbs favor. To double up on the favor of our New-South risotto, I'm going to supercharge my chicken stock by adding both dried porcini mushrooms and portobello stems, then reducing it by about 25 percent. For more flavor still, I'm going to sauté the mushroom caps in the vitamin G produced by rendered bacon (Italian cuisine is rich in the meat of that singular animal, the pig, so it's not a stretch to add a little bacon to the mix).

In Italy, risotto is usually served between the appetizers and main dish, but here in Pensacola, I like it as a meal with just a salad and, of course, some wine. A Marietta Cellars Old Vine Red is great with risotto.

Photo: Gary McCracken

Risotto Barracks Street

2 quarts chicken stock

5 cups chopped portobello mushroom caps (about 8) with stems reserved

2 ounces dried porcini mushrooms

4 large strips bacon

1½ cups Superfino Arborio rice

6 tablespoons butter

2 shallots, diced

1 cup white wine

1 tablespoon chopped parsley

1 teaspoon chopped fresh thyme

....

Remove stems before chopping portobellos. Bring chicken stock to a boil; add portobello stems and porcini mushrooms. Reduce liquid to 1½ quarts. Chuck the bacon into a skillet and cook on medium low until almost done. Remove bacon from pan to cool, but leave the vitamin G. Add portobello caps and sauté until most of the liquid has come out of the mushrooms. Remove and reserve; chop bacon and reserve.

In a medium sauté pan, cook shallots in 2 tablespoons butter for 2 or 3 minutes (till clear). Add rice and bacon and run on medium heat for 3 minutes. Don't let the rice brown. Now splash the white wine in and cook until most of the liquid evaporates, stirring the whole time. Remove porcini mushrooms from stock and reserve; strain out stems and discard. Start ladling the hot chicken stock into the pan, at first just enough to cover the rice. Keep stirring as that is absorbed. Now and then, add a bit more stock so you always have a low simmer going on. Stir, stir, stir. In about 16½ minutes, when the last of the stock has been absorbed, toss in the portobello and porcini 'shrooms and let them go for 5 or 6 minutes. When the rice is chewy but not too firm in the center, toss in the thyme, parsley and remaining butter. Stir a bit. Now it's time to pour up the red wine.

PORCINI SMASHED POTATOES

In the midst of one of my exhaustive California sojourns, I stopped in Sonoma County to see my good friend Chris Bilbro, Marietta Cellars owner and winemaker. While sipping newly released 2001s (keepers, all), I noticed large bags of dried mushrooms sitting about the winery.

"Boletus," Chris said. "You know: porcini."

It turns out that porcini grow wild on his Mendocino mountain ranch, and he invited me to go with him to collect a few.

There, the porcini only grow beneath what Chris called the "tan oaks" and some sort of tree with peeling red bark called "matron." Underneath the trees, we looked for heavy thatch from fallen leaves, then for small bumps in the thatch — a telltale sign that porcini were growing beneath. We found a couple of giant porcini and about 100 mushrooms too small to harvest, though Chris said they would grow to be giants in four days.

I donated my giant mushroom to the Rose Pistola restaurant in San Francisco, where they prepare it about 10 different ways. The chef, Tiny, brought me porcini soup, porcini wrapped in prosciutto, porcini baked on pizza, porcini salad and my favorite, porcini smashed potatoes.

Collecting wild mushrooms shouldn't be undertaken without the help of an expert and your attorney. I was assured that recent famous deaths from mushrooms resulted from getting smaller mushrooms mixed up with death caps. In the South, we've never had this problem with okra or tomatoes, but telling the difference between edible and poisonous mushrooms requires a superior acumen. My recommendation: Go with store-bought dried porcini.

Porcini Smashed Potatoes

4 pounds red potatoes, skin on
2 ounces dried porcini mushrooms
½ pound butter, unsalted

1 garlic clove, crushed
5 ounces heavy cream
1 tablespoon kosher salt

½ teaspoon white pepper
1 bottle Marietta Cellars Zinfandel

Cover potatoes with cold water in a big pot and turn on high. Pour yourself a nice glass of Zinfandel to reward yourself for procuring the mushrooms, no matter where you found them.

While potatoes are boiling, break mushrooms into small pieces and place in a small saucepan. Cover mushrooms with 1½ cups hot water and let soak for about 20 minutes. After soaking, bring water and mushrooms to a boil and reduce liquid by ½, about 10 minutes. Add butter and garlic and cook for 5 minutes. Add heavy cream, salt and pepper and cook for 5 minutes more.

Check potatoes by sticking a knife into one. If it goes into the potato easily, they're done. Drain the water. Using a potato masher, crush potatoes until smooth. Now add the mushroom-and-cream mixture to the potatoes and stir.

GRANDMA'S SOUTHERN-FRIED OKRA

As a child, I spent many great days in the summertime at my grandparents' farm outside Atlanta. Playing in the creek, riding the ponies — and best of all, eating Grandma's cooking. One of my favorite dishes was, and still is, fried okra. Trouble was, there was a catch. I had to pick the okra. Okra's defenses are prickly stalks that leave the harvester with an itch to scratch, and there were always ants or wasps waiting to sting me. Despite the obstacles, it was always worth the sacrifice.

Grandma's Southern-Fried Okra

1 pound fresh okra

4 strips bacon

1 egg

1 cup buttermilk

1 cup finely ground blue cornmeal

1 cup all-purpose flour

2 teaspoons kosher salt

2 teaspoons white pepper

2 teaspoons onion powder

2 teaspoons garlic powder

1 cup peanut oil

Grandma's cast iron skillet

1 bottle The Stump Jump (white) from
   d'Arenberg Winery

Better have a sip of The Stump Jump to relieve the pain from your trek into the okra patch. Flip bacon into your grandma's cast iron skillet and cook on medium till done. Leaving the vitamin G in the pan, fork the bacon out and pat dry between paper towels. Mince the bacon. Break the egg into a bowl with the buttermilk and beat thoroughly. Slice the ends off the okra, chop into ½-inch pieces, and plunge them into the buttermilk mix. Stir the flour and meal together with the seasonings and minced bacon. Tong the battered okra into a clean bowl and cover with flour mixture. Use a fork to separate the pieces and to coat them evenly. Add peanut oil to the bacon drippings in the skillet and set on medium high. Carefully slip some of the okra into the hot oil. Be sure to leave space around the pieces so they will crisp up. When browned, scoop out with a slotted spoon and drain on paper towels. Repeat till they're all cooked. Call in the hungry, pour up the stump juice and hunker down to some good, old-fashioned Southern vittles.

BROCCOLI ESTESS

Every day, you get an opportunity to learn from others. If you're not too caught up being an adult, you often get a chance to learn from the younger generation.

Not too long ago, I had one of these learning opportunities while dining at the home of my good friend George Estess. While George was grilling steak, his 11-year-old son, Clayton, whipped up some broccoli and Brussels sprouts that were hot enough to make me sweat, but Clayton ate them like a champ. His dish really set off the steak. So get out your wok and make this delicious side dish.

Broccoli Estess

Your favorite steak
1 head of broccoli
1 pound Brussels sprouts
10 cloves garlic
½ cup olive oil
2 teaspoons Alessi Fra Diavolo sauce or 2 teaspoons red pepper flakes
Salt and pepper to taste
1 bottle Class Shiraz

Break the broccoli into florets; slice the stems thin. While you're heating up your grill, crush and peel the garlic. Purée garlic in a blender along with the oil, a pinch of salt and 3 or 4 cranks of your pepper mill. Pour the purée into a wok with the Fra Diavolo (or red pepper flakes), broccoli and sprouts. Toss thoroughly.

Fire off your steaks and crank your wok to high heat. After 3 minutes or so, toss your vegetables again, put a lid on, lower heat and cook for 3 more minutes. The broccoli and Brussels sprouts should offer a slight resistance when bitten into; they shouldn't be soft or overdone. Add more salt and fresh-ground pepper to taste; remove from heat. Move veggies up the sides of the wok so they can drain; cover until the steaks are done. Serve with the Shiraz and toast to a lesson well-learned.

SIMPLY SQUASH

When summer arrives, a great bounty of local produce rolls into Pensacola from nearby farms. I've always enjoyed this simple recipe for fresh crookneck squash. It's quick, easy, foolproof and great for family gatherings or just a light lunch. The remaining broth is too tasty to throw out, so I always have it on the side. And if you don't finish everything off, pack leftovers into a casserole dish and refrigerate. Next day, top with bread crumbs and cheese and pop into a 425-degree oven till hot.

Simply Squash

5 or more young crookneck squash, coarsely chopped
1 large Vidalia onion, diced
1 quart chicken stock
1 tablespoon salt
1 tablespoon bacon drippings
¼ pound butter
¼ cup chopped green onions
Salt and pepper to taste
1 bottle Turnbull Sauvignon Blanc

Crack a bottle of Turnbull Sauvignon Blanc to cool down from the trip to the farm. Pour chicken stock into a medium-size pot on medium heat. Break out a sharp knife, dice up your onion fairly fine, scrape into the pot, then start on the squash. When the chunks of squash reach the top of the chicken stock, you have done enough. Pitch in the salt, give it a stir and cook for 30 minutes. Use a colander to drain the squash; set the hot broth aside. Tumble the squash back into the pot; spoon in the bacon drippings and butter. Simmer for 3 minutes, stirring occasionally. Season to taste with black pepper and maybe a bit more salt. Ladle broth into cups and garnish with green onions. Spoon squash into bowls. Pour up a glass of Turnbull for yourself and your lunch partner, offer a toast to the hardworking farmers, and fall to.

SOUPS

SLOW-COOK CHILI

I have adapted this recipe for the slow cooker from a chili recipe garnered from Los Chili Heads, a nomadic tribe made up of artists, ad guys and a lone archaeologist. The tribe migrates through Pensacola in January for its ritualistic Chili Cooking, Hat Wearing, Knife Throwing, Hootin' 'n' Hollerin' Tequila Drank. All of this activity, apparently, is performed in conjunction with moon phases, the rhythm of tides and the culmination of an arcane arena sport.

I have, with the exception of the rituals and the ingredients, faithfully replicated the recipe here.

Slow-Cook Chili

1 4-pound pork roast

2 tablespoons salt

1 teaspoon white pepper

¼ cup cumin

½ cup chili powder

10 cloves garlic, minced

1 24-ounce can diced tomatoes

1 15-ounce can tomatoes with green chilies

1 32-ounce can Bush's chili beans

1 tablespoon Louisiana hot sauce

4 tablespoons Wondra flour

Shredded cheese

Green onions, chopped

1 bottle of tequila (Cabo Wabo is just fine)

1 case of cold beer (Lone Star)

Texas toast, for sopping

The night before your party, place the roast in the slow cooker. Sprinkle salt, pepper, cumin and chili powder over the roast. Add garlic and tomatoes; put the lid on and refrigerate. Next morning, remove from fridge, turn on high, call your closest chili-head friends, invite them for supper and take off for work.

That evening, start out with shots of tequila to get yourself and your buddies into a chili-cooking state of mind. Wash the tequila down with Lone Star. (Lone Star is hard to find; any Texas beer will do.) (OK — any beer will do.)

Now turn to the chili. Keep the heat up, and use tongs or long forks to shred the pork in the pot. Stir in beans and hot sauce. Sprinkle the Wondra flour over the chili as you stir. Stir for about 5 minutes. Taste the chili and adjust your seasonings. Have another round of tequila and beer while the beans heat through.

Set out bowls for all your friends, ladle the chili, garnish with shredded cheese and green onions. Share the bread and dig in. Then polish off the tequila and beer, and in no time at all you'll find yourselves wearing hats, throwing knives and hollering at the moon.

SHRIMP AND CRAB FILÉ GUMBO

If you were to ask about one dish that runs through every family's repertoire of recipes in Pensacola, I believe you will find that it's gumbo. This rich, hearty soup can be made from any meat at hand, and beyond that, it generally should have filé or okra (or both) as ingredients, but disagreements about what goes in the pot can lead to serious trouble between families. I'm not looking for trouble, but here is a savory crab and shrimp version for your family to try.

Photo: Gary McCracken

Shrimp and Crab Filé Gumbo

7 pounds heads-on shrimp, peeled; reserve shells and heads

3 pounds crabmeat

8 bay leaves

2 cups olive oil

1½ cups all-purpose flour

3 pounds white onion, diced

7 ribs celery with leaves, diced

⅓ cup minced garlic

½ cup minced shallots

1 pound red bell peppers, diced

1 pound poblano peppers, diced

1 pound green bell peppers, diced

3 pounds okra, chopped

3 pounds tomatoes, diced

¼ cup paprika

¼ cup ground oregano

¼ cup whole thyme

2 tablespoons ground thyme

1 teaspoon cayenne pepper powder

¼ cup filé powder

1 tablespoon black pepper

2 tablespoons salt

1 tablespoon lemon peel, minced

3 ounces Worcestershire sauce

1 bottle Turnbull Sauvignon Blanc

Get your biggest pot out of the cupboard and throw in the shrimp shells, heads and 2 bay leaves. Cover with water. Boil for about 15 minutes, then strain off the shells and heads. You should have about a gallon of shrimp stock; if you are over, leave on high, reduce to 1 gallon and reserve.

While the stock boils, heat a cast iron skillet to medium high, pour in 1½ cups olive oil, add flour and start stirring. About the time you can't stir anymore, the roux will turn a nice chocolate brown for you. Set aside. Don't splash any on your skin; it sticks and burns like napalm.

Pour the remaining olive oil (½ cup) and toss the onions and celery into a large sauté pan set on medium high and sauté till they start to brown. Add garlic and shallots and sauté for 2 more minutes; then dump in the peppers, okra and tomatoes and sauté for 3 minutes. Shake in the paprika, oregano, thyme, cayenne and filé, sauté for 3 more minutes, then tumble the lot into the shrimp stock and crank up to high. Toss in the lemon peel and the remaining bay leaves (6) along with shrimp, crabmeat, Worcestershire, black pepper and salt; bring to a boil. The roux should still be hot; start drizzling and stirring it into the stock. Be sure to keep stirring about now to get the mix right. Turn the heat to low and let the whole batch simmer for 3 hours or so, stirring occasionally.

Get out some hot sauce and some French bread for sopping, pour up the Turnbull and call in the troops. But to me, gumbo tastes better the next day. So you can let it cool a bit, make room in the fridge and call in the troops tomorrow. Re-heat slowly and stir frequently; don't ruin the batch by burning the bottom.

CALLALOO, SOUTHERN-STYLE

Callaloo is to Trinidad what gumbo is to New Orleans. It's a spicy soup (a few versions I've tried just about melted my spoon) traditionally made of callaloo leaves (taro leaves), okra, peppers, pork and crab. In Trinidad, you'll find five or six versions of callaloo, each one slightly different from the other. My version uses collard greens instead of callaloo leaves — hard to find around here — and fewer habaneros. Add more if you like it hot.

Callaloo

1 3-pound Boston butt	2 cups collard greens, chopped
½ pound picked crabmeat	1 cup sweet potatoes, diced
1 tablespoon salt	1 cup okra, chopped
6 turns black pepper	1 red bell pepper, seeded and sliced
10 cloves garlic, minced	½ habanero chili pepper, seeded and minced
1 medium onion, diced	2 cans coconut milk
2 cups water	1 bottle White Haven Sauvignon Blanc
4 bay leaves	

Rub pork with salt, black pepper and garlic. Place pork in a slow cooker, cover with the diced onion and 2 cups water, add bay leaves and cook on high for 6 hours. Remove pork, add collard greens, sweet potatoes, okra, red pepper and habanero. Shred ½ the pork and add to pot. (Save the remainder of the pork for tomorrow's barbecue sandwich.) Cook for 1 hour on high. Spend the time whipping up a batch of your favorite cornbread. Add crabmeat and coconut milk to the soup. Simmer for 10 minutes.

White Haven Sauvignon Blanc is an excellent wine to accompany spicy food, so serve your guests a bowl of Southern-style callaloo soup along with a glass of chilled White Haven and a chunk of hot cornbread.

PENSACOLA MINESTRONE

Pensacola is famous for fishing, but just a bit north of the coastline it's all about farming. The array of produce available in the spring and summer is prodigious: tomatoes, potatoes, butter beans, black-eyed peas, greens of all types, cucumbers and a profusion of zucchini and other squashes. Taking a cue from the folk in Tuscany, I've knocked together some of our local produce into a minestrone soup. Just as in Italy, every area's minestrone reflects the local terrain; mine is loaded with all the fresh vegetables available from nearby farmers. It goes well with a bottle of Russiz Superiore Pinot Grigio and a loaf of Italian bread.

Pensacola Minestrone

1¼ cups fresh butter beans
1¼ cups fresh black-eyed peas
2 medium potatoes, diced
2 quarts chicken stock
2 large onions, diced
2 medium carrots, diced
2 stalks celery with leaves, diced
2 tablespoons chopped garlic
1 teaspoon red pepper flakes

4 cups collard greens, chopped
2 vine-ripe tomatoes, peeled and diced
1 cup chopped cauliflower
2 medium yellow crook-neck squashes, sliced
Fresh-ground black pepper
Kosher salt
Grated Romano from Sweet Home Farm
Extra-virgin olive oil
1 bottle Russiz Superiore Pinot Grigio

Chuck the beans, peas and potatoes into a pot with the chicken stock and bring to a boil. Simmer for 30 minutes, or until potatoes are done. Divide beans, peas, potatoes and the stock into 2 equal portions; purée 1 portion and recombine in soup pot.

In a dab of olive oil, sauté onions, carrots and celery until soft. Add garlic and cook for 2 minutes. Scrape into soup pot, pitch in red pepper flakes, collards and tomatoes, and simmer for 30 minutes. Add cauliflower and squashes; cook for 15 minutes. Add salt and pepper to taste. Garnish with grated Romano and drizzle with olive oil. Set the table, call in your company, break out the Pinot Grigio and a loaf of Italian bread and chow down.

NEW BRUNSWICK SUMMERTIME STEW

There used to be a great little barbecue joint called Melear's up near Newnan, Ga. They raised hogs on the farm next to Aunt Jo's. I loved their Brunswick stew; rich in pork, corn, tomatoes and potatoes, and seasoned with barbecue sauce. It made a kind of leftover barbecue stew that is a staple in barbecue joints in those parts.

I always assumed the stew originated in Brunswick, Ga., but over the years I've learned that both recipes and claims of origin are plentiful.

The old-school recipes called for squirrels (which I never acquired a taste for) and corn. As humorist Roy Blount says, Brunswick stew is what happens when small mammals carrying ears of corn fall into the barbecue pit.

In spite of the hot weather, summertime is a great time to make Brunswick stew because it is the best time to get locally grown vine-ripe tomatoes, lima beans, okra and sweet corn. I've made a version that's tasty, yet light. That fresh sweet corn makes all the difference.

New Brunswick Stew

1 3½-pound chicken, quartered
5 ounces diced tasso
2 medium onions, diced
5 ears sweet corn, shucked
3 bay leaves
2 teaspoons kosher salt
1 teaspoon whole peppercorns
1 tablespoon minced garlic

2 large potatoes, diced
2 large vine-ripe tomatoes, diced
4 okra pods, sliced crosswise
1 cup fresh lima beans
1 teaspoon fish sauce
2 tablespoons soy sauce
1 teaspoon wasabi powder
1 bottle Trevor Jones Virgin Chardonnay

Crack a bottle of Trevor Jones. Then chunk the chicken into a pot along with the tasso and onions. Cover with water. Set on high heat. Slice the corn off the cobs, reserve the corn and stick the cobs in the pot. Cook for about 40 minutes. While you're waiting, pull the cork again on the Trevor Jones; then whip up your favorite cornbread.

Pull the chicken out of the pot and throw everything else in. Don't forget the corn. Simmer for about 40 more minutes or until the potatoes and limas are tender. Remove cobs. Pick chicken off the bones, return chicken to pot, simmer for a few more minutes, add some salt and pepper to taste, and fall to with cornbread in hand.

OXTAIL SOUP

This was a childhood favorite of mine from Ma's cooking repertoire until I realized that the name was an actual anatomical reference. As an adult, I've gained new respect for this old-world fare.

Oxtails have a lot of flavor, and this is a great way to cook them. They're inexpensive and create a naturally thick and robust winter soup.

Oxtail Soup

3 pounds oxtails, about 1-inch cuts

1 tablespoon kosher salt

1 teaspoon white pepper

1 fistful general-purpose flour

10 shallots, minced

6 tablespoons minced garlic

4 bay leaves

2 inches ginger, ¼-inch slices

1 teaspoon red pepper flakes

2 portobello mushrooms, sliced

4 tablespoons soy sauce

1 bunch cilantro, minced

2 cups chopped spinach

2 cups chicken stock

1 bottle Marietta Cellars Zinfandel

Sprinkle oxtails with salt and pepper and dust with flour; sear (brown the meat but don't cook through; about 5 minutes in a toaster oven or hot skillet). Place in bottom of a slow cooker; pack shallots and garlic around them. Add bay leaves, ginger and pepper flakes. Cover with mushrooms. Sprinkle soy sauce, cilantro and spinach into pot, pour in chicken stock and put a lid on it. Set on high and head to work.

When you get home, fire up a batch of sushi rice.

Marietta Cellars makes a Zinfandel that's a little fruit bomb of flavor. While your rice is cooking, open a bottle and pour. Set out bowls of rice, ladle on the stew, and if you have kids, tell them it's braised beef.

ROASTED RED PEPPER SOUP
With Roasted Chicken and Poblano Cream

When the weather can't quite make up its mind, I believe that's a good time to start making the kinds of soups that are good in any weather. A rich chowder is great for icy days, but when the sun is poking out a little, roasted red pepper soup has my name on it. A little bit of spicy cream drizzled on the top will really set this soup off. Add a glass of Marietta Lot No. 36 (or another of Marietta's Old Vine Red series) to make it perfect.

Roasted Red Pepper Soup

1 chicken breast, roasted and diced

6 red peppers, roasted, peeled, seeded and chopped

1 medium white onion, diced

1 tablespoon minced garlic

2½ cups chicken stock

1 cup heavy cream

1 cup sour cream

1 tablespoon Louisiana hot sauce

1 poblano pepper, seeded and chopped

1 tablespoon sherry

1 pat butter

Olive oil for frying

Salt and pepper to taste

Blacken the red peppers under a broiler. Turn until all sides are blistered. Reserve in a paper bag and close it so the peppers steam while cooling down.

Chuck the diced onion into a deep saucepan with a bit of olive oil and sauté till translucent. Scrape off the blackened outer layer of the roasted peppers, rinse clean, seed and chop. Toss blackened peppers and garlic in with the onions and sauté for 2 minutes on medium high. Pour in the chicken stock and bring to a boil, reduce heat and purée. Add the heavy cream, hot sauce and chicken; allow to settle together on medium heat for a few minutes. Taste for seasoning. Put your poblano and sour cream in a food processor, purée till fine, then funnel the sauce into a squirt bottle.

Swirl a pat of butter and the tablespoon of sherry into the soup. Ladle into a couple of bowls and write your name and your guest's on the top of the soup with the poblano cream. Pour wine for yourself and your guest and toast the weather, whatever it is.

SCALLOP THREAD SOUP

I enjoy cool winter evenings beside a roaring fire, but to really warm your bones, nothing beats a bowl of hot soup. I got the idea for this soup from a dim sum chef in Manhattan. The trick is to boil the scallops an improbable hour; they begin to get tough in a few minutes, but when they cook an hour, they change from hockey puck to the tender threads that make this such a savory broth. Alvear Fino En Rama, a single-vintage wine produced and bottled in Spain, adds subtle nuances to this soup — not to mention you'll only need ¼ cup, which leaves plenty for sipping.

Scallop Thread Soup

½ pound sea scallops

1 clove garlic, minced

6 cups chicken stock

1 inch ginger cut into thin slices

¼ cup Alvear Fino En Rama or a good sherry

1 pinch white pepper

2 tablespoons cornstarch stirred into 2 tablespoons cold water

2 ounces tasso, chopped fine

2 tablespoons chopped basil

2 green onions, sliced very thin

Toss scallops into a saucepan with the ginger, garlic and chicken stock and bring to a boil. Cover and cook on low boil for 1 hour. Fish out ginger and scallops; reserve scallops and discard ginger. Stir in the cornstarch slurry while soup is still boiling. Cook for 2 minutes. Roll scallops between your fingers and they will break into threads. Scatter them back into the mix, then drop in the white pepper and ¼ cup of Fino En Rama. Garnish with tasso, basil and green onions. Finish a book in front of the fire while sipping Fino En Rama and relishing the soup.

SOUPED-UP VICHYSSOISE

While I was still in school, I attended a banquet in a swank ballroom in Atlanta. The first course was vichyssoise, a classic soup made with potatoes and leeks, and served chilled. Our table's server, Charles, was obviously new to the biz, but working hard at it. I asked him what the soup was.

"I don't know, sir, but I'll find out."

He was back in a flash with the news that it was vichyssoise. I asked him what vichyssoise was.

"I don't know, sir, but I'll find out."

A minute later he came back with a pained expression on his face. "Cold potato soup, sir."

"Really?" I replied.

"Yes sir, and this is such a nice place, too."

When the entrée was served with a stuffed baked-potato half as a side dish, I couldn't help asking Charles where the other half of my potato was. He looked very embarrassed and said, "I think they made the soup with it."

You should make the soup, too. I've added a little bit of the pig for my version. A bowl of this and a glass of Trevor Jones Virgin Chardonnay is truly a comfort.

Souped-Up Vichyssoise

4 slices applewood-smoked bacon

¼ pound butter

1 onion, diced

2 leeks, chopped

1 medium potato, peeled and sliced thin

3 cups chicken stock

1 cup heavy cream

Salt and pepper to taste

1 bottle Trevor Jones Virgin Chardonnay

Photo: Gary McCracken

To get a head start on comfort, crack the Chardonnay. Fry the bacon in a large saucepan with low heat so it won't brown the pan much. Chop the bacon, set aside, pour off the vitamin G left in the pan. Reserve. Wipe the pan clean so it won't color the soup. Chuck the butter, onion, leeks and vitamin G into the pan and sweat (not brown) them for about 10 minutes, then throw the potatoes and spill the chicken stock into the pan, bring to a low boil and cook for 30 minutes. Purée the soup and mix in heavy cream. No use waiting for this good stuff to chill. Salt and pepper to taste, call in the troops, pour up the wine, ladle the soup into bowls and garnish with bacon. Serve the leftovers cold and call *that* vichyssoise.

THOM KAT KAI

Hot weather is the perfect time for refreshing Asian broths. A chef at Thai Palms Restaurant in Sacramento, Calif., taught me how to make this excellent broth, which makes a great meal all by itself. This recipe is my friend Randy Hammer's favorite.

Thom Kat Kai

1 pound boneless, skinless chicken breasts

3 cups chicken stock

4 inches fresh ginger, unpeeled, sliced in $1/8$-inch pieces

2 limes

2 cans unsweetened coconut milk

1 tablespoon Thai fish sauce (nam pla)

2 tablespoons tamarind paste

1 stalk lemon grass, coarsely chopped

2 tablespoons sugar

1 tablespoon minced garlic

2 teaspoons crushed red pepper

5 Thai chilies

½ pound shiitake mushrooms, sliced thin

Fresh cilantro, chopped

Fresh basil, cut into ribbons

Salt and pepper

Throw your chicken in the oven with a little salt and pepper. Roast at 325 degrees till internal temperature reaches 160 degrees. In the meantime, pour chicken stock into a pot, turn on medium high, bruise ginger with the back of a knife to release flavor, and toss into pot; squeeze limes into pot and pitch the rinds in. Add coconut milk, fish sauce, tamarind paste, lemon grass, sugar, garlic, red pepper and Thai chilies. Bring to a boil and simmer for half an hour. Dice chicken into ¼-inch cubes, place in bottom of a bowl, and ladle hot broth over the top. Garnish with plenty of shiitake, cilantro and basil.

UNCLE BOOM BOOM'S MOCK TURTLE SOUP

One of my favorite stories that Dad used to tell is about "Uncle Boom Boom." Dad and his friend Bob Dinsmore had gone turtle hunting on Big Creek. This entailed wading the creek, floating a washpail along for the catch and poking a long steel rod into holes in the banks in search of a tasty "cooter."

Trouble was, even though you could tell which end of the turtle you were dealing with, you couldn't tell what kind you were about to grab by the tail. Your average turtle is easygoing all the way to the soup pot, but a snapping turtle, with a neck as long as its body, a sharp beak and a mean disposition, isn't going without a fight.

There's an old wives' tale that if a snapping turtle bites you, it will hold on till thunder booms. So Dad sticks the rod in and finds the turtle. Bob sticks his hand in, and a snapper promptly latches onto his thumb. Next thing you know, Bob's swinging the turtle about, yelling "Boom boom boom!" Bob was "Boom Boom" Dinsmore from then on.

Turtles are having a tough time these days, so please don't try Dad's hunting method. Instead, toss together some mock turtle soup.

Mock Turtle Soup   Feeds a mess o' people

1 5-pound Boston butt
1 lemon, halved
1½ cups diced celery
1 cup diced carrots
3 cups diced tomatoes
1 diced turnip root
3 ounces diced tasso
½ cup brown roux
1 cup minced garlic
6 bay leaves

½ teaspoon cinnamon
1 teaspoon ground clove
1 teaspoon allspice
1 teaspoon ground thyme
½ gallon chicken stock
1 cup chopped parsley
2 cups heavy cream
½ cup sherry
Salt and pepper to taste
1 bottle Domaine Chandon Chardonnay

Photo: Gary McCracken

This one is easy. The night before you serve it, make the roux by heating ¼ cup vegetable oil till it's good and hot; whisk in ¼ cup flour, reduce heat, and stir like crazy till brown (takes about 30 minutes). Next morning, toss everything but the cream, sherry and Chardonnay into a slow cooker. (Squeeze the lemon and toss in the halves.) Set on medium heat and head out to work. When you get home, pull out the pork and give the soup a good stir. Clean excessive fat off the pork, cut into ½-inch cubes and lob back into the soup along with the cream and sherry. Bring heat up to speed, ladle soup into bowls, call in the troops, crack the Chardonnay and raise a glass to Uncle Boom Boom.

ASIAN TURKEY SOUP WITH LEMON DUMPLINGS

When I was growing up, every Thanksgiving I got caught up in the excitement of meal planning and preparation, counting the days until the family gathered at the table, eager to devour as much turkey in one sitting as possible. Afterward, my anticipation was quickly replaced by a growing dread, realizing that I was looking down the barrel of six days of turkey leftovers.

These days, however, I look at leftovers as the basis of soup making. I hope that I can give you, if not anticipation of one more good meal out of the turkey, some relief from having to do serious cooking. Try this one on Saturday; it gives you a day of rest, and you can start the prep for it as you tuck the turkey away on Thursday.

This recipe will serve a lot of people, and I think it will kill the turkey blues for a day. *Tip: For a better tasting bird, brine your turkey all night in the refrigerator. Use 1 cup kosher salt per gallon of water. Don't forget to rinse well.*

The Soup

Bones and skin of turkey

3 quarts chicken stock

2 inches ginger, sliced thin

2 tablespoons minced lemon grass

6 cloves garlic, minced

4 teaspoons soy sauce

4 shallots, minced

2 teaspoons sesame oil

¼ cup chopped parsley

¼ cup chopped cilantro

10 dried black mushrooms

½ cup chopped green onions

½ cup carrots, sliced thin

½ cup mirin or sherry

2 bottles Columbia Winery
    Gewürztraminer

The Dumplings

2 cups sifted all-purpose flour

1 teaspoon salt

1 teaspoon baking soda

1 tablespoon lemon zest

1 cup buttermilk

3 tablespoons turkey fat

Start Saturday's meal on Thursday. After dinner, pull the dark meat off the bones, toss bones and skin into a big pot with the chicken stock, ginger and lemon grass, turn on high and boil for 1 hour. Cool, strain and refrigerate.

Saturday morning, pull the fat cap off the turkey stock and warm the fat cap to use in your dumplings. In a soup pot with your stock, add garlic, soy sauce, shallots, sesame oil, parsley, cilantro, mushrooms, green onions and carrots. Bring to a boil. Add mirin, then start the dumplings.

In a stainless steel bowl, mix flour, salt, baking soda and lemon zest, then mix in buttermilk and 3 tablespoons turkey fat. Mix together and knead for 3 minutes, adding more flour to prevent sticking. Roll out till about ¼-inch thick. Cut into ¾-inch pieces, drop into boiling broth and let it roll for 20 minutes, stirring occasionally. Test a dumpling for doneness, then test 2 more for kicks. Set out bowls, call in the troops, pour up Gewürztraminer for everybody and eat up.

SALADS

Owned by the Broxson family, BJ Farms in Elberta, Ala.,
is the place to go for summer vegetables

STRAWBERRY COBIA SALAD

While making one of my many pilgrimages to the Sweet Home Farm cheese shop in Elberta, Ala., I finally stopped at the giant strawberry that I use as a landmark.

Turns out the big strawberry is a true sign of what was growing at BJ Farms — giant strawberries, sweet and delicious. It occurred to me to use them in a salad with Sweet Home Farm blue cheese and the excellent cobia that were running off the beach.

The great thing about this dish is that most of the major ingredients are fresh and local — except the bacon, of course, which, as everyone knows, comes from hog heaven.

Strawberry Cobia Salad

2 6-ounce cobia fillets

6 strips applewood-smoked bacon

2 shallots, minced

2 garlic cloves, minced

1 teaspoon red pepper flakes

1 pint strawberries from BJ Farms, sliced

¼ cup white wine

2 bunches fresh spinach

4 ounces Sweet Home Farm blue cheese

¼ cup toasted pecans

Salt and pepper to taste

1 bottle Gloria Ferrar Blanc de Noir

Open a bottle of Gloria Ferrar Blanc de Noir sparkling wine to start off this spring lunch preparation. Preheat your oven to 350 degrees. Fry bacon in grandma's skillet till crisp and set aside. Toss in shallots, garlic and pepper flakes. Sauté on medium high for 2 minutes while you chop the bacon into 1-inch pieces; add strawberries, wine and bacon. Reduce for 4 minutes. Pour mixture into a bowl for a minute while you season the cobia fillets with salt and pepper and place them in the skillet. Cover fish with strawberry mix and shove all that into the oven for 20 minutes. Arrange fillets on a plate with fresh spinach and crumbled blue cheese, garnish with nuts, pour more of the bubbly for yourself and your partner and sit down to a divine down-home meal.

FRIED GREEN TOMATOES AND PAN-FRIED TRIGGERFISH

With Yellow Tomato Salsa

A few long, hot summer days is a sure sign that local tomatoes are ripening and available in most markets. I get mine from Joe Cunningham — or as we know him, Tomato Joe.

Tomato Joe is the man for great vine-ripe tomatoes: plum, cherry and beefsteak varieties — even those beautiful yellows. Joe knows tomatoes and I know seafood, so I've tossed this delicious tomato-and-seafood salad together.

A bottle of crackling cold Sauvignon Blanc will fill the bill for refreshment.

Photo: Gary McCracken

Fried Green Tomatoes & Pan-Fried Triggerfish

2 6-ounce triggerfish fillets

1 large green tomato,
    ½-inch slices

1 cup seasoned flour (1 cup all-
    purpose flour, 1 teaspoon each
    kosher salt and white pepper, 1
    tablespoon each onion powder
    and garlic powder)

2 handfuls mesclun

1 bottle Kiwi Sauvignon Blanc

Bacon and Garlic Blue Cheese Vinaigrette

½ pound bacon, fried
    and chopped

½ cup crumbled blue cheese

1 small shallot, minced

2 cloves garlic, minced

3 ounces (¼ cup plus 2
    tablespoons) apple cider vinegar

5 ounces (½ cup plus 2
    tablespoons) olive oil

2 tablespoons bacon drippings

1 teaspoon kosher salt

5 turns black pepper mill

½ tablespoon chopped parsley

Yellow Tomato Salsa

1 vine-ripe yellow tomato, diced

1 vine-ripe red tomato, diced

1 medium sweet onion, diced

Salt and pepper to taste

On low heat fry up ½ pound of bacon in your grandmother's cast iron skillet. I like to slowly pour off the rendered vitamin-G (saving it, of course), leave the bacon residue behind and then wipe the pan clean; this makes the appearance of the food that follows just that much more fetching.

Reserve 2 tablespoons drippings for the vinaigrette. Drain bacon on paper towels; chop. Mix bacon with the other vinaigrette ingredients in a quart jar, screw on the lid, shake and set aside.

Lightly salt and pepper salsa ingredients. Sprinkle with a little of the vinaigrette and toss.

Pour remaining drippings back into the skillet and heat to medium high. Dust the green tomatoes and triggerfish with seasoned flour, toss into the skillet, and fry about 3 minutes a side, or until golden brown.

Place mesclun on a large plate and dress with blue cheese vinaigrette. Lay triggerfish across greens and top with fried green tomato slices. Drizzle salsa over all, pour the wine and enjoy a nutritious, delicious summer salad.

SCALLOP & SPINACH SALAD
With Asian Bacon Vinaigrette

You never know what will get a response from people. A healthy salad drew the largest response I've ever gotten from my Good Grits column, mostly folks asking about my health and wondering where the bacon was. This week's remedy for what ails you combines nice fresh greens with fresh scallops and a vinaigrette made with a flavorful cut of our friend the pig.

Scallop & Spinach Salad

4 jumbo sea scallops

1 pound baby spinach, rinsed and dried

8 ounces button mushrooms, sliced thin

4 tablespoons minced red onion

16 carrot batons

Salt and pepper

1 bottle Casa Lapostolle Sauvignon Blanc

Asian Bacon Vinaigrette

12 pieces applewood-smoked bacon

1 tablespoon minced ginger root

1 tablespoon minced shallots

1 cup seasoned rice wine vinegar

2 tablespoons mirin

3 ounces orange juice

2 cups olive oil

Pop the bottle of Sauvignon Blanc and pour yourself a glass. Start this recipe by breaking out grandma's cast iron skillet. Fry the bacon over medium heat; when it's done, remove, leaving the vitamin G in the pan. Chop the bacon, mince the onion, cut carrots into batons, slice the mushrooms and reserve all. Then mince the fresh ginger and shallots. Combine ginger, shallots, vinegar, mirin and OJ in a food processor and leave it alone for a second.

To set up the salad, divide the spinach onto four plates and top with equal shares of mushrooms and carrots. Begin reheating the leftover vitamin G in the skillet.

Go ahead and corral the troops and pour wine for everybody, because this goes down fairly quick. Ease the warmed-up (not too hot) vitamin G into the food processor; put the skillet back on the burner at high heat. Tumble ½ of the chopped bacon into the processor, turn it on and drizzle in olive oil. Salt and pepper scallops, drop into hot skillet and sear for 2 minutes a side. Place scallops on salads, ladle on bacon dressing and sprinkle with red onion and remaining chopped bacon. Serve.

STREGA NONA'S NUTRITIONAL VINAIGRETTE
With Grilled Veggies

In the old Sacred Heart Hospital on 12th Avenue in Pensacola, there used to be a quaint little bakery and health-food restaurant called Strega Nona's. I remember the first time I had their vinaigrette. It wasn't that the flavor made you go "wow," it was more that a little voice in the back of your head was saying "get some more of that." When I learned the basic ingredients of the dressing, I realized that it might well be a primitive sense — one that identifies what's good for you — that was telling me I needed more.

Though I never discovered the exact recipe, the mix I've thrown together tastes pretty close — at least to my 10-year-old memory of the flavor. The base is Bragg Liquid Aminos, which sounds rather frightening, but tastes a lot like soy sauce and is made from soy protein. Spike, which is a seasoning mix chock full of stuff good for you, adds more flavor. And for harmony, there's nutritional yeast, which is loaded with B vitamins. All of these groceries can be found at your friendly neighborhood co-op, Ever'man Natural Foods. On your way out of Ever'man's, cross the street to Artesana and buy a bottle of Lurton Pinot Gris white wine. Its clean, fruity taste can't be beat.

Grilled Vegetable Salad

3 cups spring greens

1 large portobello mushroom cap

1 large carrot

1 medium red onion

1 zucchini

1 small eggplant

Wheat bread slices, cut in half diagonally

1 bottle Lurton Pinot Gris

Rice Wine Vinaigrette

1 tablespoon Spike seasoning

2 teaspoons Bragg Liquid Aminos

3 tablespoons nutritional yeast

1 cup seasoned rice wine vinegar

2 cups olive oil

Photo: Gary McCracken

To make the vinaigrette, stir together Spike, Bragg Liquid Aminos and yeast with rice wine vinegar, then slowly drizzle in the oil, whisking like crazy. Now cut the mushroom, carrot, onion, zucchini and eggplant into ½-inch-thick planks, place in a shallow bowl and cover with vinaigrette. (You might want to double the vegetables in this recipe; left in the fridge, they will still taste great 3 days later.) Refrigerate for at least 1 hour.

Fire up your grill. Pop a bottle of Lurton's and have a sip (to put yourself into a healthy frame of mind). Lob the veggies onto the grill and cook for a couple of minutes on each side — enough time to etch some grill marks. Hit the wheat bread on the grill for a minute; turn once. Toss the lettuces with some vinaigrette, tumble onto 2 plates, split the vegetables between them, give 'em a couple of turns from the pepper mill and garnish with the grilled bread. Pour some more vino for yourself and your friend, toast Strega Nona's, and get down to some fine, nutritious eating that won't make you feel guilty.

TRIGGERFISH EDAMAME

Soybeans are today's magic beans. From them we get sprouts, oil, lecithin, flour, tempeh, tofu, cheese and much more. Looking to create a little soybean magic of my own, I've put together a rich seafood salad using five types of soybean products. Edamame, or "vegetable soybeans," are harvested when the beans are still green and sweet. They're available in grocery stores already shelled and cooked. Soy nuts are dried, roasted soybeans. Miso paste is made from soybeans, a grain, salt, and is aged from one to three years. Tofu is curdled soy milk. Soy sauce, such as tamari and teriyaki, is made from soybeans that have undergone a fermenting process. Combine these with one of our truly great Gulf delicacies, triggerfish; some fresh spring greens and a little Craggy Road Sauvignon Blanc and — presto — you've got yourself a magical summer salad.

Triggerfish

2 triggerfish fillets
2 tablespoons miso paste
2 tablespoons prepared horseradish
2 tablespoons sweet wine
2 shallots, minced
1 bottle Craggy Road Sauvignon Blanc

Edamame Salad

2 handfuls spring greens
1 cup cooked edamame
½ cup roasted soy nuts

Dressing

2 tablespoons miso paste
1 tablespoon tofu
1 cup water
½ cup rice wine vinegar
1 teaspoon sesame oil
1 teaspoon soy sauce
1 inch fresh ginger, peeled and grated
1 cup olive oil

Mix 2 tablespoons miso paste, horseradish, wine and shallots together. Rub the mixture into the fillets, coating them with the marinade. Wrap fillets in plastic and refrigerate for at least 2 hours; preferably overnight.

To make the dressing, use a fork to mash miso paste with tofu, then whisk into the water and vinegar. Stir in sesame oil, soy sauce and ginger. Slowly pour olive oil into mixture as you stir.

Slap chilled fillets onto an oiled pan and slide into a 350-degree oven. Bake for 12 minutes. Make a bed of greens on each plate, lay a fillet on them and sprinkle edamame and roasted nuts on top. Drizzle dressing over all, pour glasses of Craggy Road for yourself and your guest and pursue the magic.

With Crowder Pea Vinaigrette

TOMATO, BUTTER BEAN AND CORN SALAD

In Pensacola, in the early days of July, we get an abundance of the hot-weather-loving vegetables, notably Silver King sweet corn, giant vine-ripe tomatoes and waves of fresh peas and beans. One of my favorite peas is the crowder, named for the way the peas are crowded together in their pods. They are not as uniform in shape as their black-eyed cousins, but they taste better. For years, during the hot season, my family would toss a salad together with crowders. This time, I'll put the peas in the vinaigrette. A crackling-cold bottle of Seresin Estate Sauvignon Blanc will really set this light lunch off.

Tomato, Butter Bean and Corn Salad

2 pounds vine-ripe tomatoes
2 cups fresh Silver King kernels, cooked
2 cups fresh butter beans, cooked
½ cup diced red onion
3 cups cubed toasted bread
Salt to taste for tomatoes
1 bottle Seresin Estate Sauvignon Blanc

Crowder Pea Vinaigrette

2 cups fresh crowder peas, cooked
2 tablespoons chopped fresh basil
2 tablespoons chopped parsley
½ teaspoon salt
5 turns on the pepper mill
½ cup rice wine vinegar
½ lime for juice
1 cup olive oil

Early in the day, go ahead and cook your corn, beans and peas. When they have cooled off, sip on a glass of refreshing Seresin. Once a peaceful state is achieved, shake basil, parsley, salt and pepper into a small mixing bowl, add rice wine vinegar and lime juice, and whisk in the olive oil. Eat a few crowder peas to test for doneness; then maybe eat a few more. Tumble what's left into the vinaigrette and whirl with a spoon. Set aside.

Dice tomatoes into ½-inch pieces and sprinkle with a little salt. Then sling the corn, beans, onion, bread cubes and tomatoes into a big bowl and jumble them around. Stir your dressing, ladle it over the salad, then give the salad a stir. Call in the locals, pour up the wine, portion out the salad and savor a light summer treat.

GAZPACHI SALAD

Pensacola has a great sense of its own culinary history. A dish native to Pensacola is gazpachi salad (aka gaspachee salad; gauspachi salad). According to Pensacola food historian Wilmer Mitchell, local legend has it that the dish is derived from Spanish and Italian sailors enjoying fresh produce in the form of gazpacho soup, dipping their rock-hard sea biscuits into the cold broth to soften them.

I consider gazpachi to be a celebration of fresh local produce — especially tomatoes. The exact recipe varies from family to family, but the basic ingredients follow.

Photo: Gary McCracken

Gazpachi Salad

1 loaf hardtack
2 or 3 large vine-ripe tomatoes, sliced thin
¼ cup Las Brisas extra-virgin olive oil
½ cup homemade mayonnaise
2 tablespoons balsamic vinegar
1 medium onion, sliced thin
2 medium sweet green peppers, sliced thin

1 large cucumber, sliced thin
¼ cup sugar
1½ cups white vinegar
Sea salt
Fresh-ground black pepper
2 bottles Russiz Superiore Pinot Grigio

I couldn't find any hardtack in town, so I made my own. You can order it online at www.wikstromsgourmet.com or make a batch with 2 or 3 cups all-purpose flour and a little water. Knead a dough that's elastic but not sticky, roll till it's an inch thick, bake at 400 degrees till it begins to turn brown, remove and let cool, then leave in oven at 200 to 300 degrees until hard.

Cover hardtack with warm water, then weight it down so all of it softens. Dissolve 2 teaspoons salt and ¼ cup sugar in white vinegar; add cucumber slices. Refrigerate. Pour yourself a glass of Russiz Superiore Pinot Grigio.

When hardtack is thoroughly soaked, squeeze out water with a towel. Bust out the sea salt and the pepper mill and season tomato slices. Layer bottom of a 9-inch bowl with tomato; cover with a thin layer of onion. Cover onion with broken-up hardtack, a layer of mayonnaise and a layer of green pepper; then another layer of onion and tomato. Drizzle with Las Brisas olive oil and splash with balsamic vinegar. Cover with hardtack and repeat layering. Follow with 1 more layer of hardtack and the last of the tomatoes. Drizzle with oil, slosh in more balsamic vinegar, cover with plastic wrap, weight with a plate and slide into the fridge.

When chilled, call neighbors and ask them to bring barbecued chicken and Nassau grits. Break out more wine, yank the gazpachi out of the fridge, crown with marinated cucumbers and let the locals in.

NORTH BEACH CALAMARI SALAD

Dining at a restaurant in the Italian section of North Beach in San Francisco, I met its executive chef, a fellow East Coaster who enjoyed grumbling with me about West Coast seafood (no triggerfish or cobia).

However, one item from the sea served there that no one could complain about was the fresh calamari (so much nicer-sounding than squid), for the restaurant was well-known for super-fresh fried calamari with a marinara. The chef also tossed together a calamari salad with an olive tapenade for me one day that was excellent. This isn't his exact recipe, but it works for me.

Calamari

1 pound calamari, cleaned
1 lime for juice
2 Roma tomatoes, diced
2 quarts water with
  ½ cup kosher salt

1 ice bath
Freshly cracked black pepper
Kosher salt
1 bottle Russiz Superiore Pinot Grigio

Olive Dressing

½ cup pitted kalamata olives
½ cup pitted green olives
  (Shoreline Deli has good olives)
2 tablespoons capers
¼ cup red wine vinegar
½ cup extra-virgin olive oil
½ teaspoon red pepper flakes
1 teaspoon Dijon mustard

While you're having a sip of Pinot Grigio to get yourself started off on the right track, put your pot of salted water on high heat and get your ice bath ready. Then toss all the dressing ingredients into a food processor and pulse till minced. Set aside.

Cut squid into rings and halve the tentacles. Drop the whole batch into the pot of boiling water and let it go for just 1 minute. With a slotted spoon or strainer, yank out the pieces and dunk into ice water to stop the cooking. When cool, rinse, pat dry and chuck into a mixing bowl. Pour the lime juice on top; tumble in the tomatoes and olive dressing. Season to taste with freshly ground black pepper and kosher salt. Toss. Alert the troops and partake with gusto.

POULTRY

at his home in Garcon Point with his prized chickens and eggs

BOURBON CHICKEN

When it comes to Halloween treats, most people think of wax lips and candy corn. Not me. I think of chicken — Beall's Bourbon Chicken, to be exact. You see, many years ago I worked at Beall's 1860, a restaurant in an old antebellum mansion in Macon, Ga. The mansion reputedly was haunted. On my first Halloween evening there, a few of us were working a party upstairs serving Bourbon Chicken. About 10:15 I was swamped, and I realized that no one was helping me. When I protested, I was informed by a staff member that "we don't go upstairs after 10, sir — that's when they come out."

Silliest thing I ever heard. Except that the light kept going off and on in the southernmost room — the one that never seemed to get warm. A stack of glasses mysteriously crashed to the floor, and when the last guest left, I had an eerie feeling that someone was still in the room with me. Now, when Halloween rolls around, I always serve Bourbon Chicken — just in case "they" decide they're hungry.

Bourbon Chicken

2 pounds boneless chicken
   thighs, cut into 1-inch cubes
½ pound bacon
Skewers or toothpicks
2 fingers good bourbon (Basil
   Hayden's Kentucky Straight
   Bourbon Whiskey)

Marinade

8 ounces soy sauce
8 ounces average bourbon
10 cloves garlic, crushed and peeled
4 shallots, minced

Sauce

4 ounces average bourbon
1 cup orange marmalade
3 cups chicken stock
3 ounces grenadine

Marinate chicken in ½ of marinade for 2 hours. Wrap each cube of chicken with bacon, and skewer. Cook at 350 degrees for 15 minutes or till the bacon starts to crisp. While the chicken is in the oven, reduce remaining marinade with the bourbon, marmalade, chicken stock and grenadine until 2 cups remain. Use this heated sauce to baste chicken as soon as it comes out of the oven. The Basil Hayden's? That's for you.

SOUTHERN BOY COUNTRY-FRIED CHICKEN

There's a restaurant in the great Northwest called Tillman's that is famous for its fried chicken. I heard that Tillman's simmers its chicken in seasoned water before frying. Good idea, but I think if you're going to go to that much trouble, why not make some soup, too?

Country-Fried Chicken

1 3-pound chicken cut into 8 pieces
2 tablespoons olive oil
2 quarts chicken stock
2 stalks celery, chopped
1 medium carrot, diced
½ medium onion, diced
2 tablespoons parsley
1 clove garlic, minced
2 shallots, minced
2 bay leaves
1 cup panko (Japanese)
    bread crumbs
Canola oil for frying

Egg Wash

1 egg
1 cup buttermilk

Seasoned Flour

1 cup all-purpose flour
2 tablespoons garlic powder
2 tablespoons onion powder
2 teaspoons white pepper
1 tablespoon ground rosemary
1 tablespoon salt

In a 4-quart pot, add olive oil and sauté the celery, carrots and onions till onions are clear, then add parsley, garlic, shallots and bay leaves. Sauté for 2 more minutes and add chicken stock. Bring to a boil and lower the heat. Put chicken into pot and simmer for about 15 minutes. Remove drumsticks and wings and refrigerate. Simmer the rest of the chicken for 10 more minutes. Remove from pot and refrigerate for at least 30 minutes. Reserve soup on low heat.

Whip the egg into the buttermilk. Blend 1 cup flour with garlic powder, onion powder, white pepper, rosemary and salt. Mix ¼ cup seasoned flour with bread crumbs. Coat chicken with the bread crumbs and flour mix. Dip chicken pieces into the egg wash, then back into the flour mix. Deep-fry in canola oil at 365 degrees until golden brown.

Serve with garlic mashed potatoes, toasted French bread and a crisp spring salad — and, of course, ladle out bowls of delicious chicken soup. Now, dig into some of the best Northwestern-inspired, Southern-fried chicken you've ever eaten.

MOCK TURKEY STUFFED WITH GRIEVOUSLY GOOD GRITS

After Hurricane Ivan reported in and wreaked so much havoc, Dr. Toad (Todd Williams of Toad Hollow Vineyards) came to town and threw a party to cheer up his distributors. The chicken and grits I cooked up inspired him to say, "These are grievously good grits." Hence the recipe title.

If cooking a whole turkey is too much for you, or if you are cooking for only one or two, give this easy recipe a try. Brining a free-range chicken, then stuffing after cooking makes this fairly foolproof.

Photo: Gary McCracken

The Bird

1 free-range chicken (Bailey's
   Farmers Market)
1 quart water
1 cup kosher salt
1 tablespoon minced garlic
1 teaspoon thyme
1 teaspoon dried basil
1 teaspoon white pepper
1 can beer
1 bottle Toad Hollow Chardonnay

The Grits

1½ cups Dixie Lily grits
1 quart chicken stock
4 ounces butter
8 ounces cream cheese
6 cloves garlic, minced
1 cup heavy cream
1 tablespoon olive oil
1 white onion, chopped
2 poblano peppers, seeded and chopped
8 slices bacon

Stir salt into water until no salt settles. Submerge bird in brine and refrigerate for 2 hours. Preheat oven to 350 degrees. Combine garlic, thyme, basil and pepper. Pat bird dry and rub spice mixture under skin and inside body cavity. Drink ½ the beer, insert can upright into the body cavity, and place bird and can on a roasting pan so that the beer can makes a third leg. Adjust the legs to make a stable tripod support. Roast for 50½ minutes or until golden brown.

Dump grits and chicken stock into a slow cooker and turn on high with lid off. When the grits begin to reduce (takes about 2 hours) add butter, cream cheese, garlic and heavy cream, purée with wand or stir until mixed well, and continue cooking on high until grits thicken (another hour or so). Sauté onions and peppers in olive oil until soft, and reserve. Fry bacon, pour vitamin G into grits, chop bacon and stir into grits along with onions and peppers. Reduce, stirring occasionally, till the grits begin to firm up.

To serve, hold bird upright and remove can. Pour pan drippings into body cavity, then spoon grits in until packed. Open the wine, break out the carving knife and ring the dinner bell.

MAPLE QUAIL WITH NASSAU GRITS

In the woods of Northwest Florida, bobwhite quail always have been a hunter's staple. They're raised locally — at Woodbine Quail Farm in Pace. One great way to prepare the birds is to soak them for eight hours in a bourbon, maple syrup and soy sauce marinade, and then toss them on the grill. Pair them with Nassau grits (for newcomers to grits: Nassau grits are laced with an edible cut of the amazing pig, peppers, onions and tomatoes), and you've got a great appetizer. The un-oaked richness of Trevor Jones Virgin Chardonnay enhances this tasty combination.

Photo: Gary McCracken

Maple Quail with Nassau Grits

4 quail

3 cups cooked grits

½ cup heavy cream

4 strips bacon

½ onion, diced

2 tablespoons butter

1 vine-ripe tomato, diced

1 poblano pepper, diced

½ cup shredded cheddar cheese

Salt and pepper

1 bottle Trevor Jones Virgin Chardonnay

Marinade Bobwhite

½ cup soy sauce

½ cup bourbon

2 tablespoons minced shallots

1 tablespoon minced garlic

1 teaspoon minced fresh ginger

4 tablespoons maple syrup

Pack quail in a small dish, mix marinade ingredients together, pour over birds and refrigerate. Eight hours later, fire up your grits and your grill.

When the grits are done, add cream and allow to reduce, slowly. Stir it a bit now and then while you're frying the bacon over low heat in your grandmother's cast iron skillet. Remove when nearly crisp and set aside to cool. Leave the vitamin G in the pan. Tumble the diced onion into the skillet and sauté till clear. Toss in the poblano and tomato and let sauté a bit while you chop the bacon.

Pop a bottle of the Chardonnay and take a sip to relax; add cheese and butter to the grits and stir like crazy. Then chuck the chopped bacon and all the stuff in the skillet into the grits. Season with salt and freshly ground pepper and let it sit for a minute. Pull the birds out of the marinade, sprinkle with salt and pepper and toss on the grill for about 4 minutes a side. Don't let the direct fire get to them or they'll look like Wile E. Coyote in a back blast. Pull the little beauties off the grill, spoon a mound of Nassau grits onto each plate, top with a bird, pour some wine for your company and chow down.

CHOOK POT PIE WAY DOWN UNDER

Way Down Under, on the hillsides of the McLaren Vale of Australia at the Dog Ridge Vineyard, live Dave and Jen Wright, who make some of the finest Shiraz about. They also lay out a fine tucker (food): homemade snags (sausages), pâtés and a fine beef or chook (chicken) pie. Meat pies are a real staple Down Under; every bakery is loaded with sausage rolls, meat pies and pasties (pastries). Here's my interpretation of their chicken pot pie.

Chook Pot Pie

2 cups Bisquick

²/₃ cup milk

2 to 3 pounds free-range chicken

2 cups red wine

2 cups chicken stock

2 large carrots, diced

1 cup fresh corn kernels

2 stalks fresh celery with leaves, diced

1 medium onion, diced

1 vine-ripe tomato, diced

1 portobello mushroom cap, diced

3 cloves garlic, diced

1 tablespoon minced ginger

1 teaspoon oregano

2 tablespoons parsley, chopped

1 leaf fresh basil, chopped

1 poblano pepper seeded and diced

1 tablespoon soy sauce

1 tablespoon Bisquick

Salt and pepper to taste

1 bottle Dog Ridge Shiraz

Preheat oven to 350 degrees. Mix milk with 2 cups Bisquick and roll out. Make round caps with the dough, press into oven-proof soup cups and bake 15 minutes or until crust is brown. Cool, remove from cups and reserve.

Except for the Dog Ridge Shiraz and salt and pepper, chuck remaining ingredients into a slow cooker and run on high until the meat easily comes off the bones.

Remove chicken from pot, pull meat, pitch the bones out and dice the chicken. Save ½ for tomorrow's chicken salad, and add ½ back into the pot. Stir well; salt and pepper to taste. Ladle into the baked cups. Pour Dog Ridge Shiraz for yourself and your guests and serve with some Down-Under Southern hospitality.

GINGER CHICKEN
With Ginger Dressing and Tossed Greens

I fell in love with ginger salad dressing at the old Tokyo Chaya on Pensacola's Chase Street. Later, the chef at the Thai Palms Restaurant in Sacramento, Calif., showed me how to make her version, but it was quite spicy. My recipe falls somewhere in between.

Chicken

2 chicken breasts, flattened

2 handfuls salad greens (spring mix)

2 or 3 green onions, chopped, for garnish

1 bottle Grgich Hills Fumé Blanc

Ginger Dressing

3 cups olive oil

1 cup rice wine vinegar

⅛ cup plus ½ tablespoon sesame oil

1 small onion, coarsely chopped

1 large carrot, coarsely chopped

¼ pound peeled ginger, sliced thin across grain

⅔ cup soy sauce

3 stalks celery, sliced

Place wine in refrigerator.

Feed dressing ingredients into food processor until smooth.

Cover chicken breasts with plastic wrap, and beat to ½-inch thick with a mallet. Toss into a large bowl, pour dressing over the chicken and refrigerate. Marinate for 1 hour.

Heat up grandma's skillet. Open the Fumé Blanc; splash some wine into the pan. Splash some into a glass for yourself; cooking is hot work. Slap chicken into the blazing skillet. Sear for 3 minutes on each side. Build a mound of salad, lay the chicken over the top, ladle dressing over both, and garnish with green onions.

DUCK WITH CHOCOLATE SHRIMP RELISH

Chocolate has received some great press recently. A new study shows that chocolate increases your brain's endorphins, making you happy. But who cares? Most of us like it for one reason: It tastes good. So break out grandma's cast iron skillet, the big one she used for company, and let's make everyone happy.

Duck

6 duck breast halves
2 tablespoons dark miso
1 teaspoon sesame oil
1 cup olive oil
1 tablespoon garlic, minced
1 tablespoon shallots, minced
½ cup mirin wine
1 bottle Sanford Pinot Noir

Shrimp Relish

Duck renderings
½ pound shrimp, peeled, deveined and diced
½ pound tasso ham, diced
1 small red onion, diced
1 poblano pepper, seeded and diced
2 tablespoons balsamic vinegar
Salt and pepper

Chocolate Sauce

1 ounce unsweetened chocolate, chopped
1 cup orange juice
2 tablespoons sherry

Blend miso, oil, garlic, shallots and mirin. Marinate duck breasts, fat side up, in the mixture overnight in the refrigerator. Place duck, fat side up, in a large cold skillet in a cold oven and turn heat to 200 degrees; leave in oven for 1 hour. Remove duck breasts and reserve; leave renderings in the skillet. Toss all relish ingredients except vinegar into skillet and sauté for 4 minutes on medium heat. Add the vinegar and salt and pepper to taste. Remove relish from skillet and set aside.

Combine chocolate sauce ingredients in a small saucepan over low heat until chocolate melts.

Heat skillet to medium high, place duck breast halves in pan, fat side down, and cook for a few minutes — until you obtain the doneness you desire. After about 4 minutes, the meat will be medium rare or medium. Serve the duck covered with relish, drizzle sauce over the top, and open a bottle of Sanford Pinot Noir.

CHICKEN DIAVOLO

In the past I have been accused of falsely claiming not to be hungry. One such incident occurred while visiting my good friend George Estess.

While enjoying some wine with George, and recently having eaten, I declined his offer to dine with him; I wasn't hungry. He was cooking his chicken diavolo, which he had pieced together from an old family recipe and what he had learned on a trip to Italy. I did taste the chicken — strictly for professional purposes, of course.

And, as George pointed out, "tasting" half a chicken seemed excessive for someone who wasn't hungry. Perhaps, but how could I resist such a devilish temptation? The next time I'm not hungry, just throw another chicken in the skillet.

Chicken Diavolo Serves two or three (depending on how hungry you are)

1 small free-range chicken
(Bailey's Farmers Market)
Kosher salt (for brining)
2 teaspoons black pepper

10 cloves garlic, chopped
3 teaspoons red pepper flakes
2 lemons
4 tablespoons olive oil

2 bricks (wrapped in foil)
1 bottle Trabucchi Valpolicella

Cut chicken in ½ and remove backbone. Brine chicken in the refrigerator for 3 hours in a solution of 1 cup kosher salt to a gallon of water. Crack the wine to get into the Italian spirit. In a small nonstick pan, on low heat, sauté the garlic, pepper flakes and black pepper in 2 tablespoons of olive oil for 5 minutes, and reserve. Rinse chicken and pat dry. Cover with plastic wrap, and beat flat with a mallet. Stuff pepper and garlic mix under skin of chicken. Be sure to get the mix under the legs and wings. In a large, shallow frying pan, drizzle 2 tablespoons olive oil, turn to medium high and place bird in pan. Press meat by placing a flat lid or pie pan smaller than the skillet on chicken and weighting with bricks.

Cook for about 15 minutes, remove bricks, turn chicken, replace bricks, and cook for another 15 minutes. Pull out the chicken, toss it onto a serving plate, squeeze the lemons on the chicken and fend for yourself.

CHICKEN LULU

I met Miss Lulu in Atlanta several years ago. She was a big-hearted Cajun chef who put okra into just about everything she cooked. I was reminded of her recently while creating this dish. It needed a little something unusual to hold it all together, so, naturally, I added Lulu's favorite ingredient: okra.

Spice Rub

1¾ tablespoons paprika

1¾ tablespoons salt

1¼ tablespoons dry mustard

1¼ tablespoons onion powder

1 tablespoon garlic powder

½ tablespoon cumin

1 tablespoon ground thyme

1 tablespoon oregano

1 tablespoon black pepper

1½ tablespoons white pepper

Chicken Lulu

1 3-pound chicken, cut into pieces

2 tablespoons oil

3 stalks celery, chopped

1 each red and yellow pepper, seeded and chopped

½ medium yellow onion, chopped

2 tablespoons Wondra flour

½ pound Thompson's hot smoked sausage, cut into ½-inch pieces

½ pound okra, cut into ½-inch pieces

1 large portobello mushroom cap, chopped

1 cup chicken stock

1 bottle St. Supery Sauvignon Blanc

Mix all spices together and rub the chicken pieces with it. Heat the oil in a heavy 3-quart pot. When hot, brown the chicken pieces. Remove and reserve chicken. Deglaze with a splash of the chicken stock to loosen the flavorful bits left from browning. Add celery, red and yellow peppers, onion, sausage and Wondra flour. Sauté until the onions are translucent, then add remaining ingredients except chicken. Cook for 10 minutes. Add chicken to the pot and cook until meat starts to fall off the bone, 30-40 minutes. To go with your Chicken Lulu, I suggest a bottle of St. Supery Sauvignon Blanc.

SEAFOOD

Fresh mullet at Joe Patti's Seafood in Pensacola, Florida

OYSTERS EROS

If you are experiencing a chill in your romantic relationship, this recipe, when carried out in full, has had some measure of success with several of my friends.

As the Dalai Lama is fond of saying, approach love and cooking with reckless abandon. So throw caution to the wind and get started. The trick is to get the majority of the preparation done ahead of time so all your date sees is effortless action on your part.

The first step is the mise en place — the gathering of the essential ingredients to prepare your dish.

Photo: Gary McCracken

Oysters Eros

1 cup plus 1 tablespoon sake (Momakawa, an
    Asian-pear-infused sake, is my recommendation.)

2 inches fresh ginger, sliced thin

2 shallots, minced

½ pound butter, room temperature

12 large leaves fresh spinach

1 teaspoon sesame oil

12 oysters on the half shell

3 ounces prosciutto, sliced thin

½ cup chopped chives

1 loaf French bread, sliced and toasted

Variety of cheeses

Candlesticks

James Taylor, "Hourglass" CD

Flowers, bouquet of hand-picked

Transcript of your grandmother's Indian love poems

1 bottle Veuve Cliquot Yellow Label
    Champagne, ice cold

Begin heating the cup of sake in a small saucepan over medium heat, slice the ginger, and then bruise the slices with the knife's handle. Add the sliced ginger and minced shallots to sake and reduce to ⅛ cup. Remove from heat and slowly whisk in the butter, reserving 2 or 3 tablespoonfuls for the bread. Strain the liquid through a chinois and keep warm.

While the sake is reducing, wilt the spinach in a sauté pan with a tablespoon of sake and a teaspoon of sesame oil. Remove oysters from shells and wrap them in spinach and then the prosciutto; return to shells. Set oven on broil; slice bread, brush with soft butter and place on a baking sheet. Slice cheeses and arrange on a tray.

Light candles and start up your James Taylor.

Just as your date arrives at the door, slide bread under broiler. Then offer up flowers, pop the Champagne and set out your cheese tray and fresh-toasted French bread. Place oysters on a small baking pan and broil 6 to 10 minutes, or until the prosciutto starts to crisp. Drizzle with sake butter and garnish with chives.

Savor the oysters with the last of the Champagne. Read your grandmother's love poems to your beloved, lean over for a kiss, and the recipe is complete.

Quick and Easy
CRISP OYSTERS

I grew up in a typical Gulf Coast family. When we had a cookout, all the neighbors were invited. In my family, the kids were recruited to help out. After years of wearing a glove on one hand and wielding an oyster knife with the other, I felt certain that the sole reason my parents had children was to have someone around to shuck Apalachicola oysters at weekend parties. (This belief was subsequently confirmed by my father.)

There is nothing like a salty Apalachicola oyster. Raw or cooked, they hold their own with all the oysters I've eaten around the world (Australia's Coffin Bay oysters are a close second). I've thrown together a quick and easy recipe for crisp oysters. And any way you eat them, nothing goes better with oysters than crackling-cold Sauvignon Blanc (an ice-cold beer is a close second).

Crisp Oysters

1 pint shucked Apalachicola oysters
Canola oil for deep frying
1 bottle Trinity Hills Sauvignon Blanc

Batter

¾ cup flour
1 teaspoon salt
1 egg
¾ cup red ale
2 teaspoons extra-virgin olive oil
1 teaspoon finely grated lemon zest

Sauce

1 cup mayonnaise
1 tablespoon prepared horseradish
6 cloves garlic, minced
1 teaspoon salt
Splash hot sauce
1 lemon for juice

Crack the bottle of Sauvignon Blanc, but take it easy on the wine, for frying is dangerous business.

While heating 2 inches of canola oil to 375 degrees in a deep sauté pan, mix salt with flour; beat egg, ale, oil and zest together and combine with flour mixture.

Blend sauce ingredients until smooth. Roll oysters through batter and drop gently into oil, being careful not to splash hot oil on yourself. Cook a few at a time; don't crowd the pan. Fry until light golden brown, turning once. Pour yourself a glass of wine, eat all the oysters you can hold, then ring the dinner bell.

CHOCOLATE SHRIMP

Every time the fishing season gets into full swing, it reminds me that in December, on the winter solstice, I head to the home of the international artist Greg Saunders for his annual celebration. The day is important to him because from that day forward there are more hours each day to fish. At the last gathering, he wowed me with this South-American-influenced dish he calls chocolate shrimp. Even though it doesn't include bacon drippings or collards, it's fun to cook and delicious any time of the year. Broccoli and rice are great accompaniments to the shrimp.

The Shrimp

16 jumbo shrimp, peeled, deveined, butterflied
6 tablespoons flour
2 teaspoons salt
2 teaspoons coarse-ground pepper
1 pound broccoli, chopped
2 limes for juice
Cooked rice
1 bottle Casa la Pistolle Sauvignon Blanc

Infused Oil

1 cup canola oil
6 tablespoons fresh ginger, minced
4 teaspoons fresh garlic, chopped
2 habanero peppers (or another type of hot pepper), sliced thin

Chocolate Sauce

2 ounces unsweetened chocolate, chopped fine
4 tablespoons sherry
2 oranges for juice

Start by opening a bottle of an Argentinean Sauvignon Blanc such as Casa la Pistolle and grab that Gipsy Kings CD "Cantos De Amor" just to add ambiance. Start your rice.

To infuse oil with heat and flavor, sauté ginger, garlic and habanero in canola for about 3 minutes in a large skillet over medium-high heat. Remove from burner and let sit for 10 minutes. Strain off the solids and return oil to the pan.

Bring orange juice and sherry to a boil over medium heat, stir in chocolate and remove from heat. Reheat spiced oil to medium. Mix flour, salt and pepper together in a small bowl and coat shrimp with mixture. When oil is hot, sauté shrimp till brown (about 2 minutes per side). Don't crowd the shrimp. When all shrimp are browned, toss with the chocolate sauce in a separate pan.

Stir-fry broccoli for 2 minutes in the infused oil. Remove and drain. Plate the shrimp with rice and broccoli, squeeze lime over the shrimp, keep the Sauvignon Blanc close by, and surprise your guests.

SHRIMP LETTUCE WRAPS

The more things change, the more they stay the same. A friend of mine dropped off some magazines from the 1970s the other day. The news headlines have stayed the same, cars were amazingly ugly (picture Ricardo Montalban in a leisure suit next to a hot red Chrysler Cordoba) and all large cities were doomed. But in the 1973 *Gourmet* magazine, to my surprise, nestled in with the jelly rings, deviled eggs and shoo-fly pie, was one of my hip "new" dishes.

Yes, my shrimp lettuce wraps, while very cool, are not in any sense new, as it turns out. It's much like discovering America, a "new" country: The natives were here for thousands of years. I suppose it would take a bit of arrogance to imagine that the "new" dish you whipped up had not been done before by thousands of cooks. Just as clichés are clichés because they are so true, a dish that tasted so good in the 1970s still tastes good.

Shrimp Lettuce Wraps

2 pounds jumbo shrimp, peeled and deveined
Carrots, onions and peppers sliced into matchsticks
Crisp leaves of iceberg lettuce
1 bottle Trinity Hill Sauvignon Blanc

Stir-fry Seasoning

4 ounces soy sauce
6 cloves garlic, minced
2 inches fresh ginger, minced
¼ cup minced cilantro
¼ cup minced basil

Infused Oil

2 cups canola oil
½ pound ginger, minced
¼ cup sesame oil

Mix together soy sauce, garlic, ginger, cilantro and basil and set aside. To infuse the oil, heat the canola and ginger on low for 2 hours, then allow to cool; strain, mix in sesame oil and reserve.

Heat up your wok blazing hot, squirt in a tablespoon of infused oil, add a couple of teaspoons of stir-fry seasoning, then a handful of shrimp. Sauté for about 3 minutes, repeat until all shrimp are cooked, and repeat process with matchstick vegetables.

Crack that bottle of cold wine and pour everybody a glass. Serve bowls of crisp iceberg lettuce. Use lettuce like tortillas; wrap veggies and shrimp and eat as you would fajitas.

SHRIMP DUKKAH OVER FENNEL-ONION BASMATI RICE

Australia's history as an English colony really shows in the diverse foods and flavors of their culinary repertoire. While there I saw a mix of Indian, Egyptian and Asian flavors. I enjoyed the shrimp dukkah made by chef Nigel Hopkins of the Salopian Inn in McLaren Vale, just outside of Adelaide in Southern Australia. Dukkah, an Egyptian mix of nuts, sesame seeds and spices, is good for dipping your bread in along with some good olive oil, or used as a crust, as in this recipe. Crisp, crackling cold Geoff Weaver Sauvignon Blanc goes well with this dish.

Photo: Gary McCracken

Shrimp Dukkah

32 jumbo shrimp, peeled,
　　deveined and butterflied
½ cup pistachios
½ cup cashews
½ cup black sesame seeds
½ cup pine nuts
½ cup pecans
2 tablespoons kosher salt
2 teaspoons white pepper
2 tablespoons ground cumin
1 tablespoon ground coriander
¼ cup olive oil
1 lime, quartered
1 bottle Geoff Weaver Sauvignon Blanc, chilled

Seasoned Basmati Rice

2 cups basmati rice
½ cup olive oil
3 tablespoons fresh garlic, minced
4 cups chicken stock
1 poblano pepper, diced
1 tablespoon ginger powder
3 teaspoons kosher salt
2 teaspoons white pepper
1 onion, sliced, grilled, then diced
1 fennel bulb, sliced, grilled, then diced

Preheat oven to 350 degrees. On the stovetop, in an oven-safe pan with a lid, heat ½ cup olive oil to medium high. Add basmati rice and sauté till golden brown; about 8 minutes. Then add garlic and sauté for 1 minute. Stir in everything but the fennel and onion, put the lid on and shove into the oven. Bake for 30 minutes, stirring at the 15-minute mark.

While the rice is cooking, fire up the grill. Then grill onions and fennel. Yank rice out of the oven, fluff with a fork and stir in fennel and onion. Add salt and pepper to taste.

To make the dukkah, grind nuts, seeds, spices, salt and pepper in a food mill. Dip shrimp in oil, coat with dukkah, and grill for about 4 minutes, or until tails curl into a C.

Pop the Geoff Weaver, break out bowls and serve rice with shrimp on top. Squeeze lime over all and dig in.

SHRIMP-CURRY PIE

About 5:30 one chilly morning at a farmers' market in Adelaide, South Australia, I came across a lovely pastry stand filled with hundreds of beautiful "pasties" of all shapes and sizes. Deciding which one to try was made all the more difficult by the addition of savory meats to the sweet cream and fruit fillings. I chose a beautiful one with the label "Chili Cheese Kransky" that looked a bit like an éclair.

I should have taken it as a warning when a pleasant woman working the stands said with an Australian lilt, "You know how to start the morning, don't ya, love."

I think they didn't sell many of those in the mornings, for a Kransky is a type of spicy sausage, and the chili peppers must have been those tiny Thai chilies that are insanely hot. Fortunately, I was saved from permanent damage by yogurt from a nearby stand.

The pastry was delicious, however. Too bad the small savory-pie tradition in the American South is generally limited to crawfish pies in Louisiana. I think I'll start tucking all kinds of goodies into small pies. As a beginning, here's my shrimp-curry pie recipe.

Photo: Tony Giberson

Shrimp-Curry Pie

2 dozen large shrimp, peeled and deveined

Salt and pepper to taste

1 box phyllo pastry dough

1 medium red onion, diced

1 carrot, diced

2 ribs celery, diced

2 portobello mushrooms, diced

1 poblano pepper, diced

3 tablespoons butter

2 tablespoons minced ginger

3 cloves garlic, minced

2 teaspoons ground cumin

2 teaspoons ground turmeric

2 teaspoons paprika

1 teaspoon pepper flakes

8 turns black pepper mill

1 tablespoon kosher salt

1 can coconut milk

3 limes, quartered

Melted butter for brushing

1 bottle Naia Spanish White (light and refreshing)

Open the wine and pour yourself a glass for the sake of pure adult-beverage pleasure. Set your oven on 350 degrees. To make the curry, heat a medium-size sauté pan to medium, plop in a tablespoon of butter and tumble in the onions, carrots and celery. Sauté for about 5 minutes.

Dump in the mushrooms, poblano pepper, ginger, garlic, cumin, turmeric, paprika, pepper flakes, black pepper and salt. Sauté for 5 minutes. Add coconut milk and reduce until it's a thick sauce. Reserve and allow to cool. Salt and pepper the shrimp and sauté in 2 tablespoons butter for 3 minutes.

Lay out ½ a phyllo sheet. Spoon about 3 tablespoons of curry mix onto the phyllo about 2 inches from the nearest edge. Top this with 2 shrimp, each chopped into thirds, and squeeze a wedge of lime over the shrimp. Fold the right and left edges of the phyllo over the middle and roll. Seal the edge and brush top of roll with butter. Repeat 11 times. Place on a baking sheet and pop into the oven for about 10 minutes. Pour up the Naia and call in the troops.

SHRIMP EMPANADAS

Back when my father was stationed in San Diego, Calif., our family would slip over into Mexico for bad plaster statues — conquistadors, camels, cougars — and good food. One of the best things we ate were the little meat pies called empanadas. Back then, the ones we were served were filled with ground meat. I like to make them with shrimp and cheese, of course.

Start out with an ice-cold Bohemia beer to set the Latino spirit. Just to be sure, put on the Los Lobos CD, "Del Este De Los Angeles" ("Just Another Band from East L.A.").

Photo: Gary McCracken

Shrimp Empanadas

¼ pound butter
2 shallots, minced
4 cloves garlic, minced
1 pound shrimp,
   peeled and deveined
1 cup heavy cream
½ pound shredded Swiss cheese
2 green onions, chopped
   (green tops only)
Salt and pepper

Dough

1½ cups masa harina
1½ cups yellow
   self-rising cornmeal
1 cup chicken stock
1 teaspoon salt
2 tablespoons Coyote Spice
2 eggs
½ cup Crisco
Melted butter for brushing

Coyote Spice

1 tablespoon paprika
1 tablespoon chili powder
1 tablespoon cumin
½ teaspoon cayenne
½ teaspoon ground thyme
½ teaspoon ground oregano
1 teaspoon salt

To start, mix coyote spices together, then make the dough. Throw all the dough ingredients, except the melted butter, in a bowl and mix till your arm hurts. When your arm really aches, toss the mixture onto a floured board and divide into a bunch of 1½-inch balls. Cover and set aside.

For the filling, heat a skillet to medium, add ¼ pound butter and sauté shallots and garlic for about 2 minutes. Season shrimp with salt and pepper, toss into the skillet and sauté until the tails curl. Scoop shrimp out and set aside. Now pour in the heavy cream and allow to reduce by ½. When you are done on the stovetop, set your oven to 375 degrees and dice the cooled shrimp.

Start putting your pies together by flattening the balls of dough into thin pancakes about 6 inches across. Use flour as necessary to keep things from sticking. In the center of each pancake place a small pile of diced shrimp, a bit of Swiss cheese, green onions and a teaspoon of sauce from the skillet. Fold in half like a turnover and seal by pinching the outer edges together. The tines of a fork work well for this and the resulting pattern looks nice, too. Place finished pies on a greased cookie sheet, brush with melted butter and bake for 13½ minutes.

PANKO SHRIMP

I love the spring. Winter has faded, the Japanese magnolias are in full, showy bloom, and the warming Gulf of Mexico brings the promise of a bountiful harvest of our favorite seafood: Gulf shrimp.

With that in mind, it seems like a good time to try one of my favorite Asian-influenced Gulf Coast shrimp recipes. It features Japanese bread crumbs, which, when deep-fried, make an exceptionally crisp, light coating.

Photo: Gary McCracken

Panko Shrimp

2 pounds jumbo shrimp,
   peeled and deveined
3 cups canola oil
1 cup panko (Japanese) bread crumbs
Deep (10-inch) pot
Frying thermometer
1 or 2 bottles Madfish Bay Chardonnay

Seasoned Flour

1 cup all-purpose flour
1 teaspoon kosher salt
1 teaspoon white pepper
1 teaspoon garlic powder
1 teaspoon onion powder

Egg Wash

1 egg
1 cup buttermilk

Orange Shrimp Sauce

1 cup orange marmalade
1 teaspoon prepared
   horseradish
1 teaspoon soy sauce

Blend your flour mixture. Whisk the egg and buttermilk for 1 minute. Dredge shrimp in seasoned flour, dip in egg wash and roll in panko bread crumbs. Coat the shrimp generously by pressing into the crumbs. Place on paper towels and refrigerate for 30 minutes. (Chilling helps prevent grease from saturating the batter.)

Heat oil to 370 degrees. While the oil heats, stir together the marmalade, horseradish and soy sauce in a small pan and slowly warm on stovetop.

Pour yourself and your guests glasses of the un-wooded Chardonnay. With its tropical fruit flavors, it goes great with this fried shrimp and orange sauce. Spoon the orange sauce into dipping bowls and set the table.

Drop shrimp a few at a time into the hot oil. In about 40 seconds they'll pop up, golden brown. Remove with a slotted spoon and drain on paper towels. Repeat until all shrimp are cooked. Pour another round of wine for everybody. Sit down and enjoy the feast.

GULF COAST PUTTANESCA

When I was living in San Francisco, I became friends with the chef at El Fiorna's. We would sip Valpolicella and talk about classic Italian fare. His favorite was a delicious West Coast version of spaghetti puttanesca, which is made with anchovies. Because some people find anchovies too strong, I've substituted a Gulf Coast favorite: shrimp stock. Any pasta is great with this sauce, but spaghetti squash is a refreshing, tasty substitute.

Gulf Coast Puttanesca (Serves 4)

3 dozen shrimp

1 large spaghetti squash

1 28-ounce can San Marzano whole peeled tomatoes

3 cups shrimp shells

3 cups water

4 Fra Diavolo peppers (available whole in oil at Artesana, downtown Pensacola) or 2 teaspoons red pepper flakes

2 tablespoons minced garlic

3 tablespoons extra-virgin olive oil

¾ cup coarsely chopped kalamata olives

3 tablespoons capers

1 tablespoon dried oregano

¼ cup chopped parsley

¼ cup grated Romano cheese

1 bottle Valpolicella Superiore from Terre del Cereolo

Peel and devein shrimp; reserve 3 cups of shells. Boil squash for 20 to 30 minutes or until fork goes in easily. Halve, scoop out and discard seeds; reserve squash in warm oven. Drain tomatoes and reserve liquid; chop the tomatoes. Boil shrimp shells, water and liquid from the tomatoes for 15 minutes; strain and return liquid to pan. Add pepper, garlic and olive oil. Reduce on medium heat for 8 minutes; add tomatoes, kalamatas, capers, oregano and parsley. Bring to a boil. Donate a splash of your wine to the mix. Toss in a dozen shrimp and cook until pink, and tails curl. Add 12 more, then 12 more, fishing out the shrimp as soon as they're done.

When liquid is reduced to sauce consistency, remove from heat, place a cup of spaghetti squash on each plate, ladle sauce over top and garnish with 9 shrimp per plate; sprinkle with Romano cheese. Pour glasses of wine all around, and appreciate the intense fragrance and hearty flavor of this Pensacola rendition of a traditional Italian dish.

CRAWFISH ÉTOUFFÉE

When Mardi Gras rolls around in Pensacola, crawfish seems to be the order of the day. If you happen to spot one of the Mardi Gras krewes parading by your place, make their day by "tossing" them a bowl of crawfish étouffée. This dish is best when cooked with the help of a krewe of four good friends — let's call 'em the Krewe of Mise en Place.

Photo: Gary McCracken

Crawfish Étouffée

2 pounds crawfish tail meat
2 cups chicken stock
2 cups diced onion
2 cups diced celery
3 shallots, diced
½ pound butter
1 cup diced green pepper

½ cup diced red pepper
1 cup green onions, diced, plus
   ¼ cup for garnish
10 cloves garlic, minced
1 cup heavy cream
1 tablespoon Worcestershire sauce
¼ cup paprika

1 cup flour
1 teaspoon oregano
¼ cup Louisiana hot sauce
¼ cup parsley, chopped
¼ pound grated Romano for garnish
2 bottles Trevor Jones Virgin Chardonnay
Mardi Gras beads

Besides yourself, this recipe requires the coordinated efforts of 4 more celebrators. Start by opening a bottle of Trevor Jones Virgin Chardonnay. Pour for all, pass out the beads, put on the Neville Brothers' "Treacherous" CD and cue up the first cut, "Mardi Gras Mambo," to set the étouffée mood.

Team up 3 of the Krewe of Mise en Place to dice the onions, shallots and celery to get them in a large pot as quickly as possible. Sauté with ¼ pound of butter. While they're cooking, ask for friendly hands to dice the peppers and green onions, chop the parsley, grate the Romano and mince the garlic.

The fourth soul gets to make the roux. Melt ¼ pound of butter over a medium fire. Mix in the flour; stir like crazy. Keep stirring till your arm's about to fall off; that's usually when the mix will turn brown on you. Watch out; if you splash any on bare skin, it sticks like napalm. When it's the color of peanut butter, remove from heat, and reserve. Pour some more wine for yourself and your friends.

When the onions are translucent, toss in red and green peppers, garlic, paprika, oregano and 1 cup diced green onions. Sauté for about 3 minutes. Now throw the crawfish tails, hot sauce, Worcestershire and parsley into the pot. Sauté for 2 minutes. Add the chicken stock and simmer the crawfish mixture for 10 minutes. Then drizzle the roux into the pot, stirring rapidly, for 3 minutes, then pour in heavy cream and keep stirring. Let this simmer on low for about 10 minutes to combine flavors. Stir in ¼ cup of the wine you're drinking — or some cooking sherry if you just can't part with the Virgin.

Pour wine for all, serve up the étouffée in big bowls with rice, garnish with green onions and Romano, and set out some Louisiana hot sauce. Laissez les bon temps roulez!

GRITS À YA YA

In 1998 I developed this Fish House favorite during the Mardi Gras season. Mardi Gras, properly celebrated, can sometimes last for days. Recognizing the toll this marathon celebration had on my friends, I created this fare that not only provided sustenance but tasted great, too. Since then we've whomped up about 50,000 dishes of my favorite child. Enjoy it at home with this recipe. Serves 4.

Smoked Gouda Cheese Grits

1 quart chicken stock
1 cup heavy cream
1 pound Dixie Lily grits
¼ pound butter
1 pound shredded smoked
   Gouda cheese

The Ya Ya

8 strips applewood-smoked
   bacon, diced
1 tablespoon minced garlic
1 tablespoon minced shallots
3 tablespoons butter
White wine
1 pound peeled and deveined
   jumbo shrimp

1 portobello mushroom cap, sliced
¼ cup diced scallions
2 cups chopped fresh spinach
2 cups heavy cream
3 cups smoked Gouda cheese grits
   (recipe at left)
Salt, pepper and hot sauce to taste

First, make your grits. Run the chicken stock into a thick-bottomed saucepan and turn on high till it boils. Mix in the grits and stir like crazy. Reduce to a simmer and allow to cook for 40 minutes, stirring occasionally. Add cream if you need more liquid. Then tumble in the butter, drizzle in the rest of the cream and stir till it's all in the family. Then shake in the shredded cheese and stir very well till it's all nice and smooth.

While your grits cook, bring a large saucepan to medium heat. Add bacon and cook for about 3 minutes, then add garlic and shallots. Sauté and then add butter and a splash of white wine. When the butter is half melted, add the shrimp. When the downsides of the shrimp become white, flip them and add mushrooms, scallions and spinach. Sauté for 2 minutes. Remove the shrimp. Pour in heavy cream and let simmer while stirring. When reduced by one third, add salt, pepper and hot sauce. Return shrimp to the sauce and combine. Spoon the sauce and shrimp onto heaping mounds of cheese grits.

DIVINE HONG KONG CRAB CAKES
With Gingered Butter

On a visit a couple of years ago to Manhattan's Upper West Side, I made friends with the sous chef at Neo, a very shishi sushi bar. He made some great crab cakes that had a wonderful Asian flair, but to me they didn't taste Japanese. "Are these Thai?" I asked. He replied that no, he was from Hong Kong, and that the cakes were his own recipe. Of course. We toasted his creations with some great chilled sake called Ginga Shizuku (Divine Droplets) served from beautiful blown-crystal sake carafes. (It was fortunate that I had taken my car title with me — those drops were not only divine, they were expensive.)

Divine Hong Kong Crab Cakes

1 teaspoon Worcestershire sauce
1 teaspoon fish sauce (nam pla)
1 teaspoon soy sauce
1 egg, beaten
1 tablespoon mayonnaise
½ teaspoon Dijon mustard
1 pound crab-claw meat
   picked of shell

6 saltines, crushed
2 tablespoons green onion, finely diced
2 tablespoons fresh basil, minced
2 tablespoons fresh mint, minced
2 tablespoons cilantro, minced
2 tablespoons lemon grass, minced
1 bottle Ginga Shizuku (Divine
   Droplets) sake

Gingered Butter

1 cup inexpensive sake
¼ pound butter, room
   temperature
1 tablespoon minced shallots
1 tablespoon minced
   fresh ginger root
Salt and white pepper

While making the gingered butter, have a sip of Divine Droplets to prepare for the delicate chopping to come. Reduce the inexpensive sake in a small saucepan with the shallots and ginger until almost all the liquid is gone. Remove from heat and whisk in butter. Strain and reserve.

Chop and mince herbs; pick shell from crab claws. Mix Worcestershire, nam pla, soy sauce, egg, mayo and mustard together. Add broken-up crab-claw meat, sprinkle with the herbs and mix well. Fold in cracker crumbs and form into eight 2-inch cakes. Wrap in plastic and refrigerate for 1 hour. Bring a nonstick pan to medium heat, spray with cooking oil and sauté cakes on each side until golden brown. Drizzle with warm (but not hot) gingered butter and serve.

GRILLED GROUPER AND ASPARAGUS

With Orange Vinaigrette

If you find yourself in California during April, be sure to add the San Joaquin Valley to your itinerary, where you'll find the town of Stockton and its annual asparagus festival. There you can get asparagus cooked 70 different ways or, as we say in the South, six ways from Sunday. If I were cooking at the festival, this is what I'd serve: recipe No. 71, Grilled Grouper and Asparagus.

So let's start our own festival. Grab your asparagus costume, fire up your grill and open a bottle of Madfish Bay Chardonnay.

Grilled Grouper and Asparagus

4 grouper fillets

2 pounds fresh asparagus, woody bases trimmed

1 large carrot in large juliennes

1 large portobello mushroom, ³/₄-inch slices

1 large onion, ½-inch slices

1 tablespoon olive oil

Sea salt

Fresh-cracked black pepper

2 bottles Madfish Bay Chardonnay

Orange Vinaigrette

2 cloves garlic, minced

1 shallot, minced

1 cup orange juice

Zest of 1 orange

¼ cup red wine vinegar

¼ cup balsamic vinegar

1½ teaspoons light soy sauce

1 teaspoon salt

8 turns pepper mill

2 teaspoons Dijon mustard

1 cup extra-virgin olive oil

Western Australia's Madfish Bay Chardonnay is perfect for the mild taste of grouper. It is un-oaked, which brings out the herbaceous odors of the fruit, including sweet-tart apple flavors. Pour glasses all around to get that festival spirit going.

Make the vinaigrette by mixing all ingredients but the oil; then drizzle oil in while whisking briskly. Reserve.

While a large pot of water starts to boil, salt and pepper grouper fillets, coat with ½ of the vinaigrette and let sit for 5 minutes. Blanch asparagus for 2 minutes; toss with olive oil, sea salt and fresh-cracked pepper. Grill for 3 minutes. Grill carrot, mushroom and onion slices about 5 minutes. Grill fillets for 3 minutes on each side; the flesh will flake when ready.

Layer vegetables on plates, place hot fillets on top and drizzle with the remaining vinaigrette. Call your guests to the table, refresh their glasses, put on your favorite asparagus music and enjoy a delicious grouper and asparagus salad.

RED SNAPPER WITH FIGS, BACON AND PECANS

Figs aren't normally ready for picking in the Pensacola area until late June or early July. Yet in May a friend of mine brought me, from an apparently enchanted tree in Warrington, a bag of ripe figs. Go figure. Immediately after eating the whole bunch, it occurred to me that figs would go great with red snapper — which were in season. I couldn't wait six more weeks for the normal fig crop, so I went to Bailey's Farmers Market for fig preserves. Well-chilled Martin Codax Burgans Albarino, a dry Spanish wine with hints of honeysuckle, goes well with all seafood.

Red Snapper with Figs, Bacon and Pecans

2 snapper fillets, 6 ounces each

6 strips applewood-smoked bacon

2 shallots, minced

2 cloves garlic, minced

1 teaspoon red pepper flakes

4 ounces fig preserves

¼ cup white wine

¼ cup toasted pecans

Salt and pepper

1 bottle Martin Codax Burgans Albarino

Pour yourself a little wine to acclimatize yourself to the kitchen. Set your oven on 350 degrees, then break out a cast iron pan and fry the bacon. When it's done, fork it out of the pan, set aside to drain, and toss in shallots, garlic and red pepper flakes. Sauté for 2 minutes over medium heat while chopping the bacon into ½-inch pieces.

Put the ¼ cup of white wine and the fig preserves into the pan, along with the chopped bacon and pecans, and reduce for about 4 minutes. Pour the mixture into a bowl and reserve. Season both sides of the fillets with salt and pepper and place in the pan. Cover fish with fig mix and slide into the oven for 20 minutes.

Serve with your favorite rice and the last of the Albarino.

VIDALIA-CRUSTED REDFISH WITH BUTTER-BEAN GRAVY

While at college in Georgia, I met a girl who once had been the Vidalia Onion Queen in Vidalia, Ga., home of my favorite sweet onion. Tracy still harbors a grudge against me for revealing her royal lineage to our classmates.

Sometimes Vidalia onion farmers have a rough go of it during harvest because of bad weather, and the onions don't even last long in the marketplace during a good year. Hurry up and get yourself a bunch of Vidalias when the season comes around, and if you find yourself in possession of a legal-size redfish, here is a tasty twist on a fish fry.

To complement this dish, I suggest a bottle of Starvedog Lane Chardonnay. (Honestly, that's its real name. I didn't make it up.) This is a nice wine from Australia, with citrus notes and a slight creaminess. So, toast the onion queen and start frying some onions.

Vidalia-Crusted Redfish

4 6-ounce redfish fillets

¼ cup olive oil

1 pound Vidalia onions

2 cups panko (Japanese) bread crumbs

1 tablespoon minced basil

1 tablespoon minced parsley

1 cup seasoned flour

1 or 2 lemons, quartered

1 bottle Starvedog Lane Chardonnay

Seasoned Flour

1 cup all-purpose flour

1 tablespoon salt

2 teaspoons white pepper

1 tablespoon onion powder

1 tablespoon garlic powder

Egg Wash

1 cup buttermilk

1 egg

Butter-Bean Gravy

1 tablespoon chopped garlic

1 tablespoon chopped shallots

1 tablespoon or so olive oil

3 cups butter beans, cooked

1 quart clam broth

3 leaves fresh basil

Sliver the onions and fry in hot olive oil till crisp. Set aside on paper towels for about an hour. This gives you time to prepare the gravy and other mixtures and time to savor another glass of Starvedog Lane.

Mix seasonings with flour and set aside. Whip your buttermilk and egg together in a shallow bowl and reserve.

To make the gravy, sauté garlic and shallots in olive oil, then add to butter beans and purée. Transfer to a sauce pan, add broth and basil leaves; cook and stir for 10 minutes on low heat or until gravy thickens.

Toss panko bread crumbs, fried onions, minced basil and parsley together in a mixing bowl.

Preheat oil in a sauté pan to medium heat. Dredge redfish fillets through seasoned flour, then the egg wash; press into bread-crumb mixture, forming a crust on the fish. Sauté until golden brown.

Set out 4 plates. Ladle about ½ cup of butter-bean gravy onto each plate and top with fillets. A squeeze of lemon and you have a dish fit for a queen.

CARAMEL-FIG WAHOO WITH MAQUE CHOUX

Mom's house in Gulf Breeze has two fig trees. The one on the east side produces lots of ripe figs, and the other one, the smaller tree on the west side, shows promise for eventually producing some truly remarkable figs.

My brother is usually lucky, beating the birds to the first crop, but I'm afraid I lost the second round to the birds. So the day's harvest of nine figs from the east-side tree was just barely enough to make my caramel-fig sauce. (This sauce is great on wahoo, but it also works well on pancakes.)

Photo: Gary McCracken

The Wahoo

4 6-ounce Gulf wahoo fillets
Green onions for garnish
Salt and pepper
1 bottle Caymus Conundrum

Caramel-Fig Sauce

1 cup orange juice
1 cup chicken stock
1 cup mirin
2 ounces sherry
1 cup minced figs
1 tablespoon soy sauce
¼ teaspoon white pepper
2 cloves garlic, minced

Maque Choux

4 strips bacon
$1/3$ cup diced yellow onion
3 ears sweet corn, kernels cut from cob
$1/3$ cup poblano pepper
$1/3$ cup diced red bell pepper
2 cloves garlic, minced
Salt and pepper
$1/3$ cup diced green onions

For this puzzling, yet delicious, mix of Asian and Southern cuisine, crack a bottle of Conundrum from Caymus Vineyards to help you see your way.

Make the maque choux first. Fry up four strips of bacon in your grandma's cast iron skillet; chop bacon and set aside. Sauté yellow onion in skillet for a minute or so. Add corn, peppers and garlic. Stir for about 3 minutes, pitch in bacon bits, cook for 1 more minute and season to taste with salt and pepper. Toss with green onions and reserve.

To make the sauce, sweep everything into a saucepan and reduce to about 1 cup. I start on high and bring the temperature down as the liquid reduces.

Salt and pepper fillets, coat with sauce and chuck into the oven at 425 degrees for about 8 minutes, or until the flesh flakes with a fork.

To plate, make a bed of maque choux, place wahoo on top, drizzle with sauce and garnish with green onion. Call in your company, pour wine all around and sit down to a delicious Southern summer treat.

SNAPPER VERACRUZ À LA PENSACOLA

I once worked in Baton Rouge, La., with a Mexican chef who had a high regard for himself and his culinary skills. One of the dishes he was most proud of was his version of an olive-tomato seafood combination called Veracruz. One day his grandmother, Maria, who worked in the restaurant rolling wonderful tamales, called me over and presented me with a plate of food. She nodded her head and said "Veracruz" in a knowing way that told me what she was really saying was, "He may be my grandson, but he doesn't know a thing about Veracruz." She was right. I was treated to a dynamite dish that made her grandson seem like a shoemaker.

I have attempted to replicate Maria's dish with our great local red snapper. But I'll be watching over my shoulder in case the grandson is somewhere around.

Snapper Veracruz à la Pensacola

4 fillets red snapper

1 dozen shrimp

Shells from shrimp

Tomato water

3 cups water

Seasoned flour (1 cup all-purpose flour, 2 tablespoons each garlic powder and onion powder, 2 teaspoons white pepper, 1 tablespoon each ground rosemary and salt)

2 tablespoons minced garlic

1 medium onion, diced

4 tablespoons extra-virgin olive oil

1 28-ounce can San Marzano whole peeled tomatoes

1 lime, quartered

3 bay leaves

1/8 teaspoon ground clove

1/8 teaspoon ground cinnamon

2 jalapeño peppers, seeded and diced

½ cup coarsely chopped kalamata olives

½ cup sliced green olives

1 poblano pepper, seeded and diced

3 tablespoons capers

¼ cup coarsely chopped parsley

Tortillas

1 bottle Madfish Bay Chardonnay, un-oaked

Photo: Gary McCracken

Sauté onions and garlic in olive oil till onions are clear. Pour liquid from canned tomatoes into a pot with 3 cups water and shrimp shells. Boil for 15 minutes. Strain out shells and return liquid to pot. Pitch in garlic, onions, 3 tablespoons olive oil, bay leaves, clove, cinnamon and jalapeños. Reduce on medium heat for 8 minutes. Chop tomatoes and add to pot along with kalamatas, green olives, poblano pepper, capers and parsley. Bring to a boil and add shrimp. Cook until pink and tails curl. Remove and reserve. Continue cooking sauce on low for 8 more minutes and remove from heat. Dust snapper in seasoned flour and sauté on medium high in 1 tablespoon olive oil for 3 minutes a side.

Place fillets on plates, squeeze lime over fillets, cover with sauce, top each fillet with 3 shrimp and serve with warm tortillas. Pour Chardonnay all around and offer a toast to Maria, a real chef.

RED SNAPPER TUSCANO

Red snapper is the fish that put Pensacola on the map, but it's available only during designated seasons meant to protect the species from extinction.

It has been a long stretch from the days when fleets of snapper smacks (large sailing schooners) carried hordes of Pensacola fishermen who caught boatloads of snapper with hand lines! Well, if your smack comes in with a ton of fish or just one snapper, I have a great recipe for you from my friend Nancy Ford.

With fresh tomatoes, fennel and olives, this light, healthful dish is perfect for spring. (So eat a couple of strips of bacon while preparing it so that you won't throw your system off balance.)

This dish still has enough oompf that you can drink a nice red wine with it. I recommend Sanford Pinot Noir.

Red Snapper Tuscano

1 red snapper, 3½ to 4 pounds, scaled and gutted

1 fennel bulb, sliced thin

1 cup kalamata olives, pitted

2 cups dry white wine

2 cups tomato sauce (recipe at right)

1 bottle Sanford Pinot Noir

Tomato Sauce

4 large, vine-ripe tomatoes, peeled and seeded

2 shallots, diced

2 tablespoons minced garlic

2 tablespoons olive oil

5 large basil leaves, chopped

½ cup red wine

Kosher salt

Black pepper

Photo: Gary McCracken

Crack your Pinot Noir and have a sip to get yourself into a fish-cooking attitude. While you're relaxing, preheat your oven to 350 degrees.

Splash the olive oil into a saucepan and heat to medium. Tumble in the shallots and sauté till clear. Add garlic and sauté for 2 minutes. Then spill in the tomatoes and red wine and cook for about 5 minutes or until most of the liquid is gone. Stir in the basil, season with salt and pepper and allow to cool.

Mix sauce with the fennel and olives. Place snapper in a baking dish (big enough for the fish, white wine and sauce). Pour white wine over fish and cover with sauce. Slide into the oven, let it run for 35 minutes, then whistle for the troops. Carefully transfer the fish to a serving platter and then pour the wine.

COBIA LACQUERED WITH HONEY & SWEET CHILI SAUCE

Cobia are big fish. Huge, even. So when your friends turn up with cobia they've caught, you'll need more than one way to fix them.

Over on the West Coast, the latest trend is "lacquering" fish. Around here, we call it glazing. So in keeping with the latest food trends, here's my recipe for lacquered cobia. Seasoned rice goes well with this dish, so I've included a recipe.

Photo: Gary McCracken

The Cobia

4 cobia fillets, 6 ounces each
Salt and pepper
¼ stick butter, room temperature
½-inch deep large pan
Trevor Jones Boots White,
    ice cold

The Lacquer

½ cup honey
½ cup sweet chili sauce
    (I get mine locally at C & F
    Asian Supply; orange
    marmalade works fine as
    a substitute)
1 tablespoon soy sauce
2 tablespoons prepared horseradish
Small bowl
Pastry brush or spoon

The Rice

4 cups chicken stock
2 cups basmati rice, rinsed
4 cloves garlic, minced
2 cups scallions, diced
2 tablespoons olive oil
1 teaspoon sesame oil
¼ lemon, squeezed and
    dropped into mix
1 teaspoon white pepper
1 teaspoon salt
Rice cooker

Start out with a glass of Boots White from Trevor Jones of Australia. Preheat your oven to 350 degrees.

Get your rice going in your rice cooker. Throw all the rice ingredients in and turn it on. The rice will be ready about the same time as the fish.

Season fillets with salt and pepper. Smear butter on pan to prevent sticking; place fillets in pan.

Stir the honey, sweet chili, soy sauce and horseradish in a small bowl to make a lacquer. Use a pastry brush or a spoon to coat the tops of the fillets with lacquer. Pop pan into oven for 15 minutes.

When your rice and fish are done, mound a cup of the seasoned basmati rice in the center of each of four plates, place a fillet on each, get out your fine crystal and pour the remaining wine. Ring the dinner bell for your fisherman friends.

GODDESS-BAKED FILLET OF TRIGGERFISH

I'll never forget the first time I tasted Green Goddess salad dressing. I was just a youngster dining with my dad at the Admiral Kidd, the Naval Officers Club in San Diego, Calif. To me, it was a new and elegant experience.

Today, most of our experience with Green Goddess comes from grocery-store shelves, but to find the roots of this classic, we have to go back to the 1920s. Green Goddess dressing originally was created at the Palace Hotel in San Francisco in 1923 for actor George Arliss, who was then appearing in the play "The Green Goddess." This great dressing classic still has a place on my salad today, but I like to modernize it a bit with some wasabi and soy. A refreshing Sauvignon Blanc from Beckmen Vineyards will really set off these flavors.

The Triggerfish

6 ounces triggerfish per person
Vegetable oil or Pam
Radicchio for garnish
1 bottle Sauvignon Blanc from Beckmen Vineyards

Per fillet:

¼ teaspoon soy sauce
1½ tablespoons Green Goddess dressing
1 tablespoon slivered radishes
1 lime for juice
1 handful spring mix salad greens

Green Goddess dressing

3 cloves garlic
2 teaspoons tarragon soaked in
   lemon juice for 5 minutes
1 lemon for juice
3 anchovy fillets
1 teaspoon soy sauce
1 tablespoon prepared wasabi
¼ cup chopped parsley
3/4 cup mayonnaise
3/4 cup sour cream
½ cup scallions

Photo: Gary McCracken

Place all dressing ingredients except ¼ cup scallions into a food processor and run on high for 3 minutes, occasionally scraping the sides. Add remainder of scallions and stir.

Preheat oven to 350 degrees. Grease a pan large enough to hold all your fillets. Season fillets with soy sauce, then rub with Green Goddess dressing; bake for 8 minutes or until fish flakes when pierced with a fork.

Toss salad greens with slivered radishes and Green Goddess dressing and put a handful on each plate. Place hot fillets on top, squeeze lime juice over all and garnish with 3 fingers of radicchio. Pour wine all around, toast the Green Goddess and enjoy a meal that harks back to all the fun in California during the Roaring '20s.

FLOUNDER WITH APPLES, POTATOES AND BACON

Ernst Loosen, of the Dr. Loosen Winery in the Mosel region of Germany, arrived in Pensacola a while back, bearing some interesting gifts from the old country. One, he brought a satchel of great German wines — wines that don't get a lot of airplay in this region. And two, he had a great recipe for sole (a flatfish we call flounder) with apples, potatoes and my personal favorite, bacon. This is a simple, rustic dish that even your grandma would love. It's no coincidence that this dish is perfect with the Villa Wolf Pinot Gris the good doctor brought along.

Flounder with Apples, Potatoes and Bacon

2 6-ounce flounder fillets	6 strips bacon
½ cup flour	½ apple, slivered
1 teaspoon garlic powder	2 potatoes, slivered
1 teaspoon onion powder	1 medium onion, slivered
1 teaspoon kosher salt	½ lemon
1 teaspoon black pepper	1 bottle Dr. Loosen Villa Wolf Pinot Gris

So they'll cook just right, it's important to sliver the apple, potatoes and onion as thinly as possible.

Season the flour by mixing with garlic powder, onion powder, salt and pepper. Sauté bacon in a large skillet over medium-low to medium heat until crisp. Remove bacon. Dust fillets with seasoned flour and place in skillet. Add spuds, onions and apples along the sides. Flip fillets after 3 minutes; move veggies aside to make sure the fillets have contact with the skillet. Toss the bacon in and cook for 4 minutes. Remove fish and cook bacon, onions, potatoes and apple another 3 minutes, turning occasionally.

Plate your fish with fixings alongside, squeeze lemon over the fish and enjoy a fine repast. Before the wine runs out, don't forget to toast Doc Loosen for such tasty fare.

GRILLED COBIA WITH SAKE BUTTER SAUCE

During cobia season along the Gulf Coast, if you're lucky enough to have a friend or a neighbor who is a cobia fisherman, you know what I mean when I say cobia is one of the best-eating fish in the Gulf. Fresh cobia has beautiful alabaster flesh, a hint of lemon in the flavor and is perfect for the grill.

Try this sake butter sauce to complement cobia's great flavor.

Grilled Cobia

4 6-ounce cobia fillets
Olive oil for brushing
Salt and pepper
1 bottle Trevor Jones Virgin
   Chardonnay

Sake Butter Sauce

½ pound butter, room temperature
1 shallot, minced
¼ cup heavy cream
1½ inches fresh ginger, sliced
1/3 cup Moonstone Asian Pear sake
1/3 cup seasoned rice wine vinegar

Light your charcoal or preheat your gas grill. While you're waiting, head for the kitchen and splash your sake and rice wine vinegar along with the heavy cream into a sauté pan and heat on medium.

Splatter in shallots and ginger; let this mix boil for a couple of minutes to reduce, and when most of the liquid is gone, start feeding the butter into the pan, stirring hard; if you need to, go ahead and pull the pan off the heat. The trick is to not let the butter get hot enough to separate.

Set this aside for a moment and season the cobia with salt and pepper, brush with olive oil, and toss the fillets on the grill for a few minutes or until the flesh on the heated side becomes opaque. Flip them and finish grilling until they become completely opaque and firm to the touch. Plate the fish and ladle sake butter sauce over the top. Serve with an un-wooded Chardonnay (my choice: Trevor Jones Virgin Chardonnay). Sushi rice and grilled asparagus make a great accompaniment to this dish.

CORN MUFFINS WITH TRIGGERFISH

I loved my grandma's corn muffins. They were delicious and filling and part of almost every supper. Cornbread is also great for lunch, and recently I added a coastal twist by serving these hot corn muffins dipped in butter along with fresh triggerfish and a refreshing glass of Pinot Grigio from Alois Lageder. Just for fun, I cooked my muffins in grandma's old cast iron pan with its indentations shaped like corn on the cob.

Photo: Gary McCracken

Triggerfish

4 triggerfish fillets (about
   6 ounces each)
1 lemon sliced into quarters
1 medium onion, thinly sliced
Salt and pepper
1 bottle Alois Lageder Pinot Grigio

Corn muffins

3 cups Dixie Lily cornbread mix
2 eggs
¾ cup sugar
¾ cup sour cream
½ cup buttermilk
¼ pound melted butter
Zest from 1 orange
1 cup cooked corn kernels

Orange butter

1 orange for juice
¼ pound melted butter
½ cup sugar

Preheat oven to 400 degrees. Pour yourself a splash of wine. Start by making the butter. Stir orange juice, butter and sugar together until thoroughly mixed, and reserve. Next, move on to the muffins.

Whip sugar into eggs and stir in sour cream and buttermilk. Mix in butter, orange zest and corn; gently fold into cornmeal. Butter muffin pan and fill each cup indentation with batter to just below the top of the pan. Cook 15 to 20 minutes — until brown on top. Remove from oven, dip each muffin into orange butter, pop onto a tray and reserve in a warm spot. Now for the fish.

Brush a large cast iron skillet with butter. Salt and pepper fillets and place in skillet. Top with onion slices. Splash a little Pinot Grigio on fillets, and splash a little more into your glass. Cook in 400-degree oven for about 10 minutes or until fish flakes with a fork. Crumble a muffin on each plate to make beds and plop the fillets on top. Squeeze lemon on fillets and then lace with orange butter. Place hot muffins alongside. Refresh your guests' glasses with the Pinot Grigio and sit down to a magnificent lunch.

SNAPPER POACHED IN THAI-GINGER POT LIQUOR

Some things are hard to waste. Whenever I cook up a mess of collard greens, a good bit of pot liquor is always left, even more than I can sop up with cornbread.

Pot liquor — the delicious, nutritious broth left over after cooking greens — is seasoned with the ham and onions used to flavor the greens, not to mention the flavor of the greens themselves. Pot liquor is a great base for soups and sauces.

So, with all the beautiful snapper and all the fresh collard greens available in local markets, I feel obliged to offer a way to prepare a delicious snapper meal, and, at the same time, not waste pot liquor.

In this recipe I'm turning pot liquor into a Thai-style poaching liquid. It has some exotic ingredients, but the technique is easy. Poaching is an almost foolproof method for cooking fish, and the snapper itself lends great flavor to the liquid without losing its own personality. Toss in more chilies if you like it hot. A little sticky rice contributes to the Southeast Asian twist. Crackling cold Sauvignon Blanc from Trinity Hill is a perfect beverage for this dish.

Snapper Poached in Thai-Ginger Pot Liquor

2 6-ounce snapper fillets

1½ cups pot liquor (left over from a batch of collard greens)

1 can unsweetened coconut milk

2 inches unpeeled fresh ginger, $\frac{1}{8}$-inch slices

½ lime

1 stalk peeled lemon grass, 1-inch pieces

½ tablespoon Thai fish sauce (nam pla)

2 Sanaam chilies

1 pinch saffron

1 tablespoon tamarind paste

½ tablespoon minced garlic

1 teaspoon crushed red pepper

½ pound shiitake mushrooms

Fresh lime basil, shredded

Cooked rice

1 bottle Trinity Hill Sauvignon Blanc

In a large cast iron skillet, over medium heat, combine pot liquor, coconut milk, ginger, lime, lemon grass, fish sauce, chilies, saffron, tamarind paste, garlic and red pepper. Bring to a boil. Turn to low and simmer for 30 minutes. Allow to cool to room temperature.

Place snapper fillets and mushrooms in skillet. Turn heat to medium and poach for 9 minutes. Plate by spooning rice into a bowl, placing fish on top, and pouring poaching liquid over all. Garnish with lime-basil chiffonade, pour the Trinity Hill, and fall to.

COBIA AND GOAT CHEESE ENCHILADAS

When Cinco de Mayo is just around the corner, you have a great excuse to drink Mexican beer and toast Mexican verve. The celebration also reminds me how hard it was to get Latin foodstuffs locally just a few years ago.

I had a little burrito spot back then called the Screaming Coyote, and even wholesale suppliers didn't carry the base ingredients I needed. I found one local grocer with barely a three-foot section of Latin foodstuffs, and I would clean him out two or three times a week. One day I was elated when I found that he had installed an entire row of Latin groceries.

I offered my gratitude to the manager, who told me that apparently there was a larger Latin community around than they had realized, because the store was being cleaned out two or three times a week.

Cobia and Goat Cheese Enchiladas

2 6-ounce cobia fillets, grilled

4 large flour tortillas

1 cup shredded cabbage

4 ounces goat cheese

1 cup refried beans

1 cup shredded cheddar cheese

1 case Bohemia Beer

1 package chips, your call

1 jar salsa, your favorite

CD of your favorite salsa tunes

Spicy Enchilada Sauce

2 tablespoons olive oil

2 tablespoons flour

2 teaspoons cumin

2 tablespoons chili powder

1 tablespoon minced garlic

2 cups chicken stock

½ cup diced red onion

2 pinches salt

Grill the cobia and reserve. When your guests arrive, get the music going. Set out the chips, salsa and Bohemia. Have a sip of beer to put your mind at ease.

To start the sauce, heat a small saucepan to medium, add oil and flour, and stir together about 4 minutes, or until the roux starts to bubble. Shake in cumin, chili powder and garlic and stir for 1 minute. Slowly stream in the chicken stock, stirring the whole time. As the sauce thickens, add 1 or 2 pinches of salt and sacrifice a splash of beer to the mix, toss in the onion and let simmer for about 10 minutes.

Now lay out your tortillas and place 3 ounces of cobia on each, then ¼ cup shredded cabbage, 1 ounce of goat cheese and ¼ cup refried beans. Wrap the tortillas and place in a baking dish, cover with sauce, shake cheddar cheese over the top, and bake until the cheese starts to brown and the sauce bubbles. Yank out of the oven and turn up the salsa — if your guests haven't already. Buen provecho!

PORK, BEEF, LAMB AND RABBIT

Frank Emmons, a butcher at Apple Market in Pensacola. Florida

PORK CHOPS WITH ESPRESSO REDEYE GRAVY

Back in the '70s, traversing the country in a Bonneville station wagon with my folks, I got my first taste of ham and redeye gravy at a diner somewhere in the Texas desert along Interstate 10. The waitress wasn't sure whether kids should have coffee, and I wasn't sure why she brought it up, but I assured her that, at 10 years old, I was an accomplished coffee drinker. My dad nodded. The ham was old-school — the heart-attack kind with plenty of fat and floating in redeye gravy, which was, much to my surprise, basically stale coffee. But I was hungry, and it tasted good.

I'm going to jazz up that simple fare by substituting thick pork chops for the ham, and espresso and Southwest seasonings for the gravy. Allowing refrigerated chops to warm up to room temperature and starting with a cold skillet will help keep the meat tender. Hahn Estates Syrah goes great with these chops.

Pork Chops with Espresso Redeye Gravy

4 pork chops, loin cut, bone 1 inch thick	1 tablespoon sugar	¼ cup chicken stock
1 tablespoon dark chili powder	2 turns pepper mill per side of chops	1 shot espresso
1 tablespoon kosher salt	½ tablespoon olive oil	2 tablespoons butter
1 tablespoon ground cumin	1 shallot, peeled and minced	1 bottle Hahn Estates Syrah

Tumble the chili powder, salt, cumin and sugar into a small bowl and mix. Pat this mixture onto the chops. Crank 2 turns of the pepper mill on each side of the chops. Cover with plastic wrap and let sit out for about 30 minutes. Chuck the chops into grandma's big cast iron skillet and slide onto a burner set on medium heat (if you use an electric stove, preheat the coil but not the pan). Cook 6 minutes on the first side, flip the chops, put a lid on and let them sizzle for another 6 minutes.

Pull from skillet and set aside. Drizzle olive oil into the skillet, toss in the shallot and sauté on high for 2 minutes. Pour in chicken stock and espresso and reduce by ½. Add butter, toss the chops in with the sauce, and cook on reduced heat for 2 minutes.

NINE-CHILI ENCHILADAS IN FOUR CHAPTERS

Prologue

A sure sign of summer is when friends start to show up with hot peppers from their gardens. I have revised my original nine-chili recipe for enchiladas by spreading the peppers around a bit to get a good balance. This recipe may appear to be lengthy, but it's really easy to follow. The most important thing to watch is how much habanero, cayenne and jalapeño you add. Use just a pinch of each for their unique flavors — or throw in a handful for that foot stompin', eye-poppin' steam-bath effect. An excellent wine with this dish is a Marietta Cellars Red Zinfandel.

Photo: Gary McCracken

Chapter One: Butt and Nothin' Butt

1 4-pound Boston butt
3 tablespoons minced garlic
4 tablespoons ancho chili powder

1 sliver orange or red
   habanero pepper
1 serrano pepper, seeded and diced

½ dried chipotle pepper
1 tablespoon kosher salt

Rub spices into pork, stuff into a slow cooker, add water to the ¾ mark and toss in the remaining spices. Cook for 6 hours on high. While cooking, make the sauce and salsa (recipes below). Remove pork, allow to cool and pull meat into slivers. Refrigerate stock until fat hardens into a cap.

Chapter Two: Sauced Again

½ cup seasoned fat cap
3½ cups seasoned pork stock
1 cup all-purpose flour

2 tablespoons paprika
1 tablespoon ground cumin
1 jalapeño pepper, seeded and sliced

1 cayenne pepper, seeded, sliced
1 red onion, diced

Bring fat to medium heat, add flour and stir for about 3 minutes. Toss in paprika and cumin and stir for 1 minute. Add stock, jalapeño, cayenne and onion. Cook for 5 minutes. Purée with a wand, cook for 10 more minutes, strain mixture and reserve.

Chapter Three: On the Road to Roasted Salsa

1 jalapeño pepper
2 poblano peppers
2 large vine-ripe tomatoes

1 large red onion, peeled
   and sliced thick
7 cloves peeled garlic

¼ teaspoon cumin
¼ teaspoon oregano
1 teaspoon kosher salt

Toss all ingredients on a large pan and slide into a 400-degree oven. Roast until they start to blacken. Allow to cool until you can peel, seed and dice the peppers; then dice tomatoes and onion. Mince garlic. Toss peppers, tomatoes, onion and garlic into a bowl, sprinkle with salt, cumin and oregano. Reserve.

Chapter Four: It's Thrilling with Pork Filling

4 cups pulled pork
1 large red onion, diced
3 tablespoons minced garlic
2 teaspoons dried oregano

2 tablespoons olive oil
2 teaspoons kosher salt
1 cow horn pepper, seeded, diced
1 cubanelle pepper, seeded, diced

Flour tortillas
Shredded cheddar
Chopped green onions

In a large pan, sauté onions in olive oil until translucent; then toss in oregano, garlic, salt and hot peppers. Sauté for 2 minutes, add pork and sauté for 3 minutes, mixing well.

Epilogue

To prepare for serving, put ½ cup of pork onto each tortilla, pour 1 ounce sauce over pork, roll up tortilla, place in baking pan and cover with 2 ounces sauce and 2 ounces shredded cheddar. Bake for 10 minutes. Pour Zinfandel for your family and guests, ladle salsa over top of enchiladas and garnish with green onions.

PORK TENDERLOIN MEDALLIONS ON TEXAS TOAST

My weekend grill friends have requested this recipe as an easy-to-grill pork dish. This requires use of a hot grill, so it's best that you start with ice-cold margaritas. Splash in some peach juice to get you and your friends into a Texan/Georgian state of mind.

Tenderloin Medallions

6 ounces (per person) pork tenderloin

1 tablespoon ginger powder

1 tablespoon chili powder

1 tablespoon ground cumin

1 tablespoon kosher salt

1 loaf Texas toast

¼ cup chopped cilantro

Vidalia Marmalade

1 large Vidalia onion, thinly sliced

1 clove garlic, minced

2 cups red wine

½ cup orange juice

⅓ cup tupelo honey

¼ cup homemade vinegar

1 teaspoon orange zest

½ teaspoon kosher salt

Sauté onion in a nonstick skillet until it begins to caramelize (about 8 minutes). Add garlic and sauté for 1 minute; then add 1 cup of wine and simmer for 10 minutes. Add remaining wine, orange juice, honey, vinegar, zest and salt. Simmer until reduced (about 20 minutes). Reserve. (Refrigerate marmalade if you aren't going to use it right away, but warm to room temperature before serving.)

Slice tenderloin into ½-inch medallions. Mix ginger, chili powder, cumin and salt in a small bowl. Dip each medallion in the seasonings and rub in well. Sear on the grill about 2 minutes per side. Cut Texas toast into quarters, butter it and grill for about 1 minute.

Spoon marmalade onto the toast, top with pork and garnish with cilantro. Wash down with a margarita.

PENSACOLA PORK PO' BOY

When I visit New Orleans, I always try to squeeze in a couple of sandwich stops somewhere along the way. Two of my absolute favorite places are the Central Grocery Company and Mother's. Central Grocery on Decatur Street is where you'll find the best muffuletta on the planet. And Mother's on Poydras Street is home to the Ferdi Special.

This last juicy masterpiece is a po' boy made from, among other things, debris (the local name for pieces of roast beef that have fallen into the juices while cooking). I have whipped up a version of the Ferdi that I consider a tribute to that fine sandwich. However, when I make mine, rather than beef, I use pork. And rather than just using meat that has fallen off the roast, I create a lot more "debris" by shredding all of it. It's the crusty slivers of pork that make these sandwiches taste so good.

Feeds 10 of your hungry friends.

Photo: Gary McCracken

Pork Po' Boy

4-pound Boston butt (bone in)

3 pounds spareribs

Salt and freshly ground black pepper to taste

2 large onions, sliced

1 teaspoon red pepper flakes

1 tablespoon thyme

1 cup shallots, minced

1 cup garlic, minced

1 cup Worcestershire sauce

1 cup red wine

1½ quarts beef stock

5 18-inch (approximately) baguettes from
   Pitzmann's European Bakery

5 bottles Titus Zinfandel

Well-Dressed Slaw

1 small head of cabbage, shredded

1 cup mayonnaise

1 cup brown mustard

1 cup prepared horseradish

Browned onions (from top of roast)

Preheat oven to 425 degrees. Cut Boston butt into 1-inch pieces. Place into deep pan with bones and spareribs. Salt and pepper to taste. Break up onion slices and spread over the top. Roast in oven until meat is browned; remove onions, and reserve. Flip meat over and shove back into the oven.

Chop reserved onions and set aside for the slaw. Mix red pepper, thyme, shallots and garlic into the Worcestershire sauce, red wine and beef stock. When meat has browned, pour mixture over meat, cover pan tightly with aluminum foil and reduce heat to 350 degrees. Now is the time to break out the glasses and pour the Titus Zinfandel for your friends, for you'll need to bake the meat for 2 hours.

Remove meat from pan and shred. Discard bones and unwanted fat (in my house, "unwanted fat" is an oxymoron). Strain juice. Toss meat back into the juice and let sit over low heat until ready to serve.

Make the slaw by mixing together the mayo, mustard, horseradish and onions and tossing it with the shredded cabbage.

To serve, halve and split baguettes like a hot dog bun, lay a scoop of slaw mix into the crevice, then mound with meat. Ladle hot juice over all and serve while it's good and hot.

KOREAN BARBECUE

I love barbecue. (What Southern boy doesn't?) One of the tastiest kinds I've run across is Korean barbecue.

It's usually served as a filling for those wonderful sticky buns. Piled over Grandma's Cornbread, I have found that this barbecue tastes even better than with sticky buns.

Try to find a bottle of Marietta Cellars Old Vine Red "Lot Number" series and call a friend. These wines' fresh-fruit-up-front flavors blend well with this Asian twist to a Southern staple.

Korean Barbecue

3½ pound Boston butt

3 tablespoons kosher salt

2 inches fresh ginger, sliced and bruised

10 cloves garlic, minced

3 shallots, minced

1 small onion, diced

2 tablespoons sambal oelek or red pepper flakes

2 cups water

2½ tablespoons sesame oil

3 tablespoons brown sugar

¾ cup honey

1½ cups soy sauce

1 bottle Marietta Cellars Old Vine Red

Set your slow cooker on high. Rub salt into the meat, slide into cooker and cover with ginger, garlic, shallots, onion, sambal and water. Cook overnight.

Remove lid, pick out ginger and shred pork (it will be falling apart) with a fork. Mix in sesame oil, sugar, honey and soy sauce. Ladle over hot cornbread. Pour yourself and your friend a glass of Marietta Cellars red wine.

BROWN-BAG HAM

I once worked in a restaurant in Georgia with an old Southern gentleman named Baram McIntyre, and Baram did not feel it was his job to educate those around him in the kitchen. If you asked how much or how many, he would look at you over his glasses, shake his head and say, "'If ya don't know, son, I kent hep ya.'"

He always cooked ham in a brown paper bag. When I asked him if it was to keep the flavor in, he just glared at me. He also kept a Coca-Cola nearby at all times. Sometimes he would splash a little into the sauce he was making for the ham.

"What's the Coke for?" I asked.

"If ya don't know, son, I kent hep ya," he said.

It took a long time for me to realize his Coke often was spiked with rum.

Brown-Bag Ham

1 12-pound-or-so ready-to-cook ham (the shank is my favorite)

1 pint rum

1½ cups (or more) Coca-Cola

1 large brown paper bag

About a thumb's length of fresh ginger

¾ pound brown sugar

½ teaspoon red pepper flakes

½ cup soy sauce

½ cup pineapple juice

Preheat oven to 325 degrees. Pour a shot of rum and ½ cup of Coke into a tall glass filled with ice cubes; stir and sip. Give a short toast of thanks to Baram.

Slide ham into the brown paper bag and place in a large shallow pan. Seal bag by folding closed. Cook 15 to 20 minutes per pound (3-4 hours). Don't let the bag touch the oven walls.

While the ham is cooking, slice ginger into ¼-inch pieces; bruise with back of knife (to help get the juices out). Dump brown sugar and pepper flakes into a small saucepan; pour in soy sauce, pineapple juice and a cup of Coca-Cola. Heat on medium until reduced by ½. Makes about 1¼ cups.

Remove ham from oven, leave in sealed bag and let rest for about 2 hours.

To serve: Warm up sauce. Slice ham, place on plates and drizzle with sauce. And if you don't know what to do with what's left of that rum and Coke, son, I kent hep ya.

SPARERIBS WITH BLUEBERRY BARBECUE SAUCE

My father has always had a wild passion for picking blueberries, a trait not passed on to me. I am always happy to cook with them, however. So if you're tired of cakes and pies made with fresh berries (I personally don't know when this happens), you can easily make up a batch of wild barbecue sauce. I find this goes well with a Marietta Cellars Zinfandel, so open a bottle and get started.

Meat

½ rack of spareribs for each person
Fresh-ground black pepper
Kosher salt
1 bottle Marietta Cellars Zinfandel

Sauce

¼ cup vegetable oil
5 cloves garlic, minced
5 shallots, minced
3 tablespoons ground ginger
2 pints blueberries
2 cups soy sauce
¼ cup Creole mustard
1 cup seasoned rice wine vinegar
¼ cup distilled vinegar
½ cup brown sugar
1 teaspoon cumin
½ teaspoon cinnamon
2 tablespoons Sriracha hot sauce
1 cup sweet chili sauce
1 cup water
1 tablespoon fresh-ground black pepper

Fire up your grill to medium-low heat. Rub ribs with black pepper and kosher salt to taste and toss on the grill.

In a pot large enough for all the sauce ingredients, sauté shallots, garlic and ginger in the oil for 4 minutes over medium heat. Combine remaining ingredients and purée. Add to pot and simmer for 10 minutes. Let it cool down a bit and then refrigerate.

Grill ribs until tender; this takes ¾ to 1¼ hours. Turn when necessary to brown evenly.

During the last 15 minutes, baste with blueberry sauce. Serve with potato salad, coleslaw and more Zinfandel.

FIG RUMAKI AND BEEF FILLETS

Our old house in Gulf Breeze, like many older Southern homes, has a fig tree in a corner of the yard. When summer arrives, you race the mockingbirds and blue jays to the ripe fruit. One summer my brother was the early bird, and he showed up with a basketful of nice-looking fruit. His only request was that I "throw together something for me and my friends, using the figs." That's my brother's way of saying "make sure it has bacon, cheese and beef, too."

So here's a twist on the old-school hors d'oeuvre rumaki. Substitute figs for water chestnuts, and toss on the grill with some fillets stuffed with Alabama goat cheese (made by Fromagerie Belle Chevre). Grab a bottle of Titus Cabernet Sauvignon, and you're off to the races. And remember: Fresh figs don't count in carb calculations as long as they are from your own tree.

Fig Rumaki and Beef Fillets

4 fillets of beef about 1½-inches thick
4 ounces Alabama goat cheese
8 long sprigs rosemary, plus short pieces
16 strips bacon, cooked but still soft
32 basil leaves
2 portobello mushroom caps, sliced and grilled
32 fresh-picked figs
1 bottle Titus Cabernet Sauvignon

Steak Rub

2 tablespoons paprika	1 tablespoon black pepper
2 tablespoons kosher salt	2 tablespoons onion powder
1 tablespoon ground rosemary	1 tablespoon cayenne powder
1 tablespoon celery salt	1 tablespoon dried oregano
2 tablespoons garlic powder	1 tablespoon dried thyme

Stir the steak-rub spices together thoroughly. Mix the goat cheese with a teaspoon of the rub, cut small slits in the fillets, and stuff the cheese in. Close the slits with rosemary twigs. Rub the steaks with spices, then slap them on the grill till they reach the color you favor. (About 3 minutes a side on a hot grill works for me.) Lay a basil leaf and a portobello slice on ½ strip of bacon, and wrap around a fig. Skewer with a rosemary sprig. Do this 4 times per sprig. Chuck the skewers on the grill and cook about 2 minutes per side. Pour a glass of wine for everybody, and serve the steaks with the skewers on top. You'll be happy that you beat the birds to the figs.

FILET MIGNON WITH HOMEMADE BÉARNAISE

I first made this classic French sauce as a boy while working in Beall's 1860 restaurant in Macon, Ga. My mentor, Chef Geraud, stood toe to toe with me as he tasted the sauce; then he poured it on my shoes. I was stunned.

"You must be a shoemaker," he said.

"What?" I said, just barely controlling my youthful rage.

"This tastes like shoe leather. You're not a chef, so you must be a shoemaker!"

What a beautiful insult. Looking back, I probably deserved it.

Filet Mignon With Homemade Béarnaise

4 fillets of beef, 1-inch thick
6 tablespoons white wine vinegar
6 tablespoons white wine
5 tablespoons fresh tarragon
1 minced shallot
¼ teaspoon crushed black pepper

4 egg yolks
½ pound melted butter
Pinch cayenne powder
Pinch ground white pepper
Kosher salt
1 bottle Wild Hog Pinot Noir

Slowly reduce vinegar, white wine, 4 tablespoons of tarragon, black pepper and shallot to about 3 tablespoons. Whisk yolks and a pinch of salt in a stainless steel bowl 2 minutes; then heat over simmering water 2 minutes, stirring constantly. Whisk in melted butter 1 tablespoon at a time; then, still over simmering water, whisk in vinegar reduction, the remaining tablespoon of fresh tarragon, a pinch of cayenne and white pepper. Reserve.

Rub kosher salt into the fillets. Turn on the kitchen hood fan, heat well-seasoned cast iron skillet up to high heat and drop fillets into the blazing pan. Sear 3 minutes on a side. Serve with your favorite spuds and steamed fresh asparagus. Ladle sauce over all, toast Chef Geraud and all the shoemakers you know with a sip of Pinot Noir, then relish the superior taste of homemade béarnaise.

TOP-OF-THE-HEAP CORNED BEEF HASH

Whenever I'm in Manhattan after midnight, I inevitably find myself at the Mount Olympus Diner, a small Greek restaurant, ordering from the late-night menu: corned beef hash with a poached egg on top. At the request of several New York transplants, I have started making my own. Think of them as hash browns squared.

Feeds five hungry Southerners at midnight.

Top-of-the-Heap Corned Beef Hash

1 packet corned beef (uncooked)
4 tablespoons vegetable oil
1½ pounds shredded potatoes
2 medium onions, diced
2 shallots, minced
4 cloves garlic, minced
½ cup chopped green onions
2 tablespoons Louisiana hot sauce
1 tablespoon Worcestershire sauce
10 eggs, poached
Salt and pepper to taste

Manhattan

Bourbon, 1 shot per glass
Sweet vermouth, a splash per glass
Maraschino cherries, 1 per glass
Ice

To get yourself and your guests into a big-city mood, cue up "New York, New York." Stir your bourbon, vermouth and ice in rocks glasses; garnish with a cherry.

Cook corned beef according to package instructions. Shred when done. Sauté potatoes and onions in 2 tablespoons oil till brown. Add shredded corned beef, garlic and shallots to potatoes and onions and sauté till shallots are tender. Let cool a bit and toss in salt, pepper, green onions, hot sauce and Worcestershire. Knead well.

Form into 4-inch patties and in the remaining oil sauté 3 minutes on each side. Serve with a couple of poached eggs on top and the manhattan cocktail on the side.

SLOW-BRAISED SHORT RIBS

"I am a soldier in the service of a Southern kitchen."

— Col. Bruce Hampton

Ever since relocating here from Atlanta, musician Bruce Hampton has fallen in love with our local comfort foods. He really attacked a plate of slow-braised short ribs that I cooked. He said the ribs were great and now understands the saying, "An army travels on its stomach."

This is a fairly easy version for the gourmet on the go.

Slow-Braised Short Ribs

3 pounds beef short ribs

2 tablespoons kosher salt

4 teaspoons black pepper

4 tablespoons flour

8 plum tomatoes, sliced thin

10 cloves garlic, minced

6 shallots, minced

4 bay leaves

2 teaspoons oregano

½ teaspoon red pepper flakes

2 teaspoons paprika

½ teaspoon ground thyme

1 teaspoon dried mustard

3 sprigs rosemary

2 slices stale bread, crumbled

2 cups chicken stock

2 bottles Rhône wine

Open the first bottle of wine and pour yourself a glass. Sprinkle the short ribs with salt and pepper and then lightly flour. Sear these in a toaster oven or a skillet until browned. Remember that you are not cooking the ribs, only searing the outside.

Place in slow cooker, stuff pot with tomatoes, garlic, shallots and bay leaves; sprinkle the oregano, red pepper, paprika, thyme, mustard and rosemary into the pot. Toss in the bread crumbs; pour the chicken stock and 1 cup of the red wine over all. Cover. Put the pot in the fridge.

The next morning, place the pot in the heating unit and turn to high. When you arrive home, make a batch of rice in your rice cooker, open the second bottle of wine, pour a glass for yourself and your date, fire up the fireplace and salute the good Col. Hampton and the joys of slow-cooked Southern comfort.

ROASTED PRIME RIB WITH ROASTED POTATOES

When my cuisine-challenged friends get the "someone's-coming-to-dinner-and-I-can't-cook" jitters, I send them this easy version of prime rib that my mentor, Chef Geraud of Beall's 1860 in Macon, Ga., was famous for. He'd find me trying something exotic in the kitchen, and while cussing and throwing pots at me, he'd tell me to always keep it simple. To go with this recipe, choose a bottle of Marquis Philips Merlot.

Roasted Prime Rib with Potatoes

1 3- to 4-pound prime rib of beef, trimmed ½ inch
½ cup Dijon mustard
¼ cup red wine
2 teaspoons thyme
3 cloves garlic, minced
2 pounds red potatoes, split

2 large carrots, quartered
1 celery stalk, quartered
Kosher salt
Black pepper, cracked
1 bottle Marquis Philips Merlot

While your oven heats to 375 degrees, rub kosher salt and cracked pepper into the meat. Sear it in grandma's skillet until browned. Pour yourself a congratulatory glass of Merlot.

Mix mustard, wine, thyme and garlic in a small bowl. Rub ½ the mustard mix into the meat and place in a roasting pan. Roast for 1 hour, then coat with remaining mustard mix. Toss carrots, celery and potatoes into the pan with the prime rib and cook until internal temperature is 110 degrees. Allow to rest for 10 minutes; carve the roast and impress your guests.

LAMB CHOPS STUFFED WITH BLUE CHEESE

The one constant in Easter dining with the Shirley family has always been lamb. Old school was medium-well with mint jelly; these days, we are more medium-rare, and we're stuffing it with blue cheese. I'm using the just-released blue from our neighbors at Sweet Home Farm. This buttery blue cheese with locally grown rosemary makes a delicious filler for lamb. Grab a bottle of Saintsbury Garnet Pinot Noir for a perfect match.

Stuffed Lamb Chops

2 racks of lamb
½ cup blue cheese (preferably Sweet Home Farm)
¼ cup Dijon mustard
1 tablespoon garlic
2 tablespoons fresh rosemary
2 tablespoons sea salt
Black pepper, fresh-cracked
1 cup panko (Japanese) bread crumbs
1 bottle Saintsbury Garnet Pinot Noir

Sweet Home Farm Blue Cheese Sauce

1 cup red wine
½ cup blue cheese
1 tablespoon minced garlic
1 shallot, minced
1 tablespoon fresh rosemary
1 tablespoon mustard
10 turns pepper mill
5 drops hot sauce
1 teaspoon Worcestershire sauce

Set oven at 400 degrees. Crack the Pinot Noir and have a glass for peace of mind. Mix ½ cup blue cheese with 1 tablespoon rosemary; mix mustard, garlic and remaining rosemary. Set both mixtures aside. Cut each rack in ½. Rub with sea salt, then sear on medium-high heat for 2 minutes a side in grandma's cast iron skillet. Allow to cool. Cut incision in base of lamb chop from bottom to center of chop. Stuff with blue cheese and rosemary mixture. Blanket racks with fresh pepper, rub with mustard mix and pack panko bread crumbs over all. Toss into hot oven and bake for about 45 minutes. Remove from oven, pour pan juices into a saucepan and reduce by ½ on high heat. Mix all sauce ingredients together and stir juices into the sauce. Allow racks to cool for about 10 minutes before you carve. To serve, pour a little sauce on each plate and top with sliced lamb.

Photo: Cary McCracken

DOWN-SOUTH DENVER RIBS

Some of the best foods for entertaining during seasonal holidays are dishes that have been slow cooked for richness, but only take a moment to heat and serve. This makes you look like a pro when you toss out a real jewel of a meal.

Lamb is a great holiday surprise. I've fallen in love with Denver lamb ribs (spareribs trimmed of fat and connective tissue), but they can be hard to find. Lamb shanks work well in this recipe if you can't find the ribs. An easy-drinking Pinot Noir, such as Rutz Cellars Sonoma Coast, is great for any season.

Photo: Gary McCracken

Poblano Mint Jelly

¾ cup water
4 poblano peppers,
seeded and chopped
1 cup chopped pineapple
½ cup chopped fresh mint
1 cup apple cider vinegar
1 box Sure-Gel fruit pectin
5 cups sugar

Rib Rub

1 cup paprika
1 cup sugar
1 cup kosher salt
1 teaspoon ground clove
1 teaspoon ground nutmeg
2 teaspoons cayenne
1 teaspoon ground coriander
1 tablespoon garlic powder
½ cup fresh-ground black pepper

Denver Ribs

4 racks of Denver ribs (about
   4 pounds)
2 tablespoons olive oil
1 cup chopped onion
1 cup chopped celery
1 cup chopped carrots
2 cups dry red wine
½ cup chopped tomatoes,
   peeled and seeded
¼ cup minced garlic
4 bay leaves
4 teaspoons fresh thyme
4 turns black pepper
7 cups chicken stock
1 bottle Rutz Cellars Sonoma
   Coast Pinot Noir

Make the jelly a few days before cooking the ribs. Toss into a 6-quart saucepan the carefully measured water, peppers, pineapple and mint. Pour vinegar over this, and add the pectin. Bring to a rolling boil for 1 minute, then, stirring like crazy, mix in the sugar and let go for 1 minute more. Cool quickly, pour it into a jar and refrigerate.

Throw rib rub ingredients together, and (surprise) rub ribs with it. Break out your grandmother's big black skillet, crank it up on high, then sear each rack for 3 minutes on each side. Put them into a slow cooker along with oil, onions, celery, carrots, wine, tomatoes, garlic, bay leaves, thyme, black pepper and chicken stock. Allow to boil; then turn to medium, and let it go for 2 hours.

Allow to cool, cut into individual ribs, and refrigerate with liquid over top. The day you're ready to serve, pour your guests a glass of Rutz Cellars Pinot Noir, remove ribs from liquid, and pop into a 425-degree oven for 8 minutes. Purée liquid to make a thick sauce, and warm it in a saucepan. Serve ribs with the sauce and jelly. Don't count on leftovers.

SPEZZATINO DI CONIGLIO ALLA SENAPE

Dr. Bruce McCraw, my friend and fellow gourmand, introduced me to an excellent dish he brought back from Italy, where he was cooking with the Italian chef Umberto Menghi. I've made some changes to the recipe, but the spirit remains. So not to stray too far from the Tuscan landscape, we will start with Peter Zemmer Pinot Grigio during preparation and finish with Sanford Pinot Noir for dining.

Photo: Gary McCracken

Rabbit

1½ pounds rabbit loin or boneless
   chicken thighs
3 tablespoons butter
3 tablespoons olive oil
1 bottle Peter Zemmer Pinot Grigio
1 bottle Sanford Pinot Noir

Mustard Sauce

¼ pound butter
½ cup minced shallots
¼ cup minced garlic
1 cup chicken stock
½ cup dry white wine
¼ cup Worcestershire sauce
4 tablespoons Dijon mustard
3 bay leaves
14 turns pepper mill
1 lemon, quartered
1 tablespoon blackening spice
2 cups heavy cream

Seasoned Flour

1 cup all-purpose flour
1 teaspoon salt
1 teaspoon white pepper
2 teaspoons garlic powder
1 teaspoon onion powder

Open the Pinot Grigio and pour glasses for yourself and your guests to prepare your taste buds for this treat.

Start by stirring seasonings into flour. Set aside. Then make the mustard sauce. Sauté shallots in butter till translucent; add garlic and sauté for 2 minutes. Add chicken stock, white wine, Worcestershire, Dijon, bay leaves, pepper, lemon and blackening spice. Cook for 15 minutes, strain through a chinois (or layers of cheese cloth) and reduce for 15 minutes — or until you have a little more than ¼ cup of liquid. Add heavy cream, reduce heat and stir occasionally.

As you bring a skillet to high heat, cut loins into 2-inch pieces and dredge through seasoned flour. Add olive oil and butter to skillet and sauté meat until brown — 3 to 4 minutes per side. Reduce heat to low, add mustard sauce and cook for 2 minutes, allowing sauce to coat the meat. Open the Pinot Noir (the bottle of Pinot Grigio will be empty by now) and pour glasses all around. Plate the loins and cover with sauce. Serve with roasted vegetables and bread for sopping. Toast the good doctor for bringing us this wonderful recipe.

TO FINISH

Pastries at Pitzmann's European Bakery in downtown Pensacola

CARL AND GEORGE'S EGGNOG

Christmas is the season for traditions. Some traditions are keepers, others are suspect. For me, one that belongs in the latter category is fruitcake. Nowadays this dusty relic, passed from family to family, is rarely eaten (for health reasons).

On the keeper side of traditions is eggnog, a holiday concoction enjoyed by many of our pioneering partying kin. I can skip the fruitcake, but historical eggnog is much to my liking. Our rum-smuggling forefathers added a kick to the bounty of milk and eggs available in the New World. George Washington was well known for his particularly potent mix.

I will start with some fresh eggs from Carl Wernicke's backyard, take a hint from George W. and use rum, brandy (I prefer cognac) and whiskey for the kickers (I'll follow Southern tradition and use mostly bourbon), and finish with cream and spices. If you're not getting eggs from your backyard, you might want to try pasteurized eggs.

Eggnog

12 egg yolks	2 cups sugar	5 ounces Courvoisier
1 teaspoon ground cinnamon	1 quart heavy cream	5 ounces Myers's Original Dark Rum
1 teaspoon ground nutmeg	1 cup milk	1 vanilla bean
12 egg whites	1 quart Jim Beam	

Beat egg yolks in a steel bowl with 1 cup sugar and the cinnamon and nutmeg. Then beat 1 cup of sugar into the egg whites until they reach stiff peaks. Mix the cream and milk in with the yolks, then whip in the whites. Slowly pour in the bourbon, cognac and rum. Split and scrape the vanilla bean and stir into the mixture.

Old-school recipes say let this sit for days, but after careful testing, I determined that it's best to drink it fresh. As a matter of fact, I recommend that you finish making and testing the eggnog just as your guests arrive, for continued testing beforehand can shorten the length of the gathering. So call your friends and toast the holiday and our first president. And remember; please don't nog and drive!

ICE CREAM WITH BACON

As a friend once said to me, "What doesn't go good with bacon?" Taking up the challenge, I offer you ice cream and bacon. You'll like it. Ignore taunting friends. They'll like it, too. Crumbled bacon and sweet Spanish wine makes for a surprisingly tasty topping — one you won't find at your local ice-cream parlor.

Bacon Ice Cream de Añada

1 quart whipping cream
1 quart half-and-half
2 cups sugar
1 tablespoon vanilla extract
¼ teaspoon salt
1 strip fried bacon for each person
2 ounces Alvear Pedro Ximenez de Añada per person

I use Chuck Kwasin's recipe for the ice cream. It's simple and foolproof. Pour cream, half-and-half, sugar, vanilla and salt into ice-cream maker (electric unless you have small children you can sucker into cranking). Pack with ice and rock salt. Let it whirl for about 45 minutes. That's enough time to fry some bacon until it's crisp. Press bacon between paper towels and allow to cool.

Serve by scooping ice cream into martini glasses. Crumble a strip of bacon over each dish and top with a couple of ounces of Pedro Ximenez de Añada.

BOURBON PECAN BAKLAVA

When I was a boy, my family always left Saint Nick some cookies and a glass of milk on Christmas Eve. Nowadays, my heart still goes out to the big guy for making those millions of stops while braving the cold air all night long. As thanks, and to warm him up, I leave him three fingers of Basil Hayden's Kentucky Straight Bourbon Whiskey and a little something for his sweet tooth: Bourbon Pecan Baklava. My recipe is a slightly Southern twist of the classic Greek dessert. A little bourbon and hometown pecans (J.W. Renfroe Pecan Company) give this a Pensacola flavor.

Baklava

1 pound butter (melted)
1 pound phyllo pastry sheets
    (Athens 9- by 14-inch twin pack)
1 pound Renfroe shelled pecans
1 cup sugar

Bourbon Orange Glaze

1 cup orange juice
½ lemon for juice
3 ounces bourbon
2 cups sugar

First have a sip of bourbon. This will settle your nerves and sustain your patience for the job ahead. Set your oven at 425 degrees. While it's warming up, butter a 10- by 15-inch pan. Blend the pecans and sugar in a food processor until fine. Take a pack of the phyllo from the fridge and cover with a damp cloth. Pull 1 sheet off and lay it neatly in the pan; brush lightly with butter. Repeat until all the sheets in the pack are gone. Now pour in the pecan and sugar mix and spread evenly. Start the process of neatly stacking and buttering phyllo sheets all over again. Do this until the second pack is gone, then cut into a diamond pattern and bake for 45 minutes.

Bring the orange juice, lemon juice and sugar to a boil, remove from heat and stir in bourbon. Reserve the glaze till the baklava comes out of the oven, then pour evenly over the top and allow to cool. Plate up some baklava for the jolly old elf, and don't forget the bourbon.

STRAWBERRY CRÈME BRÛLÉE

When March's crazy weather finally mellows into sparkling spring, it's time to grab the tribe and drive to Elberta, Ala., to pick fresh strawberries at BJ Farms. (While you're there, you might as well stock up on cheese from Sweet Home Farm across the way.) There's no end to the uses of fresh strawberries; in salads, pies, cakes, dumplings and even baked on fish. Here we'll use them to make a sauce — sautéed à la bananas Foster — to cap crème brûlée.

Use fresh eggs if you can find them. Carl Wernicke agreed to make a run past his insolent, rebellious rooster and score a few fresh eggs for me.

A nice "sticky" (wine slang for dessert wine), such as Alvear Pedro Ximenez de Añada, will really put this over the top.

Photo: Gary McCracken

Strawberry Crème Brûlée

2 cups heavy cream

1 vanilla bean, split

5 egg yolks from Wernicke's happy chickens

½ cup sugar

1 pint strawberries, sliced thin

¼ pound butter

1 cup brown sugar

4 ounces butterscotch liqueur

1 bottle Alvear Pedro Ximenez de Añada

....

Preheat oven to 275 degrees. Go ahead and taste the sticky to put yourself in a baking mode. When your mind's right, slide the egg yolks into a bowl with the sugar and whisk well. Pour cream into a small saucepan, scrape seeds from vanilla bean into cream and heat over medium until edges begin to boil. Remove from heat and gradually beat cream into the egg mix.

Ladle mixture into brûlée dishes and array in a large 2-inch-deep baking pan; pour hot water into baking pan until water comes about halfway up sides of dishes. Bake for about 15 minutes, or until edges are firm and middle still has some jiggle. Allow to cool for a few minutes.

To make the sauce, toss butter and brown sugar into a separate pan over medium heat. When the sugar begins to boil, splash in the butterscotch liqueur and stir hard for 2 minutes. Tumble in the sliced strawberries; remove from heat. Cover custard tops with sugar and caramelize with the blowtorch you keep in your kitchen. Ladle the sauce over the brûlée, pour up sticky for everybody and enjoy a treat that's at its best in springtime when the chickens are happy and the strawberries are fresh.

KEY LIME PIE

As in many Florida coastal towns, Key lime pie is a staple in Pensacola dining. My Georgia grandmothers made amazing crab-apple pies and cakes, but Key limes don't grow in Georgia, so they didn't make Key lime pies. I was on my own when it came to whipping up this classic South Florida dessert.

I've seen Key lime pies ranging in color from bright green to pale yellow, and there seems to be plenty of debate on the subject. My thought is this: Key limes, which are blotchy-colored little things, have a very pale juice. You're going to get more color from the egg yolks than from the lime juice.

Lore has it that lack of cows in the Florida Keys brought about the use of sweetened condensed milk. That same logic would put meringue, rather than whipped cream, on top.

Crust

12 graham crackers
¼ pound butter
3 tablespoons granulated sugar

Filling

½ cup Key lime juice
1 14-ounce can sweetened
    condensed milk
4 egg yolks

Meringue

3 egg whites, room temperature
¾ cup superfine sugar
¼ teaspoon cream of tartar

For this recipe, I recommend a power mixer (unless you have Popeye arms). Toss the crackers, butter and sugar into a food processor and run it for a minute or so. Firmly pat this mixture into the bottom and up the sides of a 9-inch springform pan, forming a crust. Bake at 350 degrees for 5 minutes and remove from oven.

Beat egg yolks till smooth. Add condensed milk and mix well; then slowly beat in the lime juice. Pour this concoction into the cooled crust and push back into the oven for 5 minutes.

While the pie cooks, throw 3 egg whites into the mixing bowl with ¼ teaspoon cream of tartar. Beat on high until soft peaks form, then add sugar a tablespoon at a time, beating till peaks get stiff. Carefully tumble and spread meringue onto the top of the pie and pop back into the oven. Bake for 7 minutes; the meringue tips will start to brown. Yank the pie out of the oven, let it cool, then crank out the cappuccinos and call in the troops.

INDEX

212

INDEX

Where Jim shops

Artesana
242 W. Garden St., Pensacola, FL 32502
(850) 433-4001
wine shop ordering (850) 433-VINO
Online: http://www.artesanaimports.com

Apple Market
1021 Scenic Highway, Pensacola, FL 32503
(850) 433-4381

Bailey's Farmers Market
4301 North Davis Highway, Pensacola, FL 32503
(850) 434-7644

BJ Farms
27618 U.S. 98 East, Elberta, AL 36530
(251) 986-5391

Central Grocery Co.
923 Decatur St., New Orleans, LA 70116
(504) 523-1620; toll-free ordering (866) 620-0174

Ever'man Natural Foods
315 West Garden St., Pensacola, FL 32502
(850) 438-0402
Online: http://www.everman.org

Joe Patti's Seafood Company
South A and Main streets, Pensacola, FL 32501
(850) 432-3315; toll-free ordering (800) 500-9929
Online: http://www.joepattis.com

Pitzmann's European Bakery
101 South Jefferson St., Suite 3
Pensacola, FL 32501
(850) 432-6026

J.W. Renfroe Pecan Company
2400 West Fairfield Drive, Pensacola, FL 32505
(850) 438-9405
Online: http://www.renfroepecan.com

Shoreline Grocery Store
1180 W. Main St., Pensacola, FL 32501
(850) 433-8852; fax orders (850) 433-1531
Online: http://www.shorelinedeli.com

Sweet Home Farm
27107 Schoen Road, Elberta, AL 36530
(251) 986-5663

Wikstrom's Gourmet Foods Inc.
5247 N. Clark St., Chicago, IL 60640
(773) 275-6100
Online: http://www.wikstromsgourmet.com